MONTESSORI
HOMESCHOOLING
ONE FAMILY'S STORY

Susan Mayclin Stephenson

MONTESSORI HOMESCHOOLING
One Family's Story

Michael Olaf Montessori Publishing Company
PO Box 1162
Arcata, CA 95518, USA
www.michaelolaf.net
michaelolafcompany@gmail.com

ISBN 978-1-879264-27-4

Establishing a lasting peace
is the work of education;
all politics can do
is keep us out of war
— Montessori, *Education and Peace*

Cover Images of War and Peace:

Background: (War) Drawing of ancient Samurai battle, by Michael
Front: (Peace) Michael and Kélé, on Moonstone Beach,
    Humboldt County, California (from an oil painting by the author)
Author: selfie taken in Trinidad, California in July, 2020

Thank you Jim, Michael,
Narda, and Ursula

TABLE OF CONTENTS

INTRODUCTION

We shall walk together on this path of life, for all things are a part of the universe, and are connected with each other to form one whole unity. This idea helps the mind of the child to become fixed, to stop wandering in an aimless quest for knowledge.

[The child] is satisfied, having found the universal center... with all things.

—Montessori, *To Educate the Human Potential*

Parents have always been and will always be the child's universal center, the most important teachers. This is how values, attitudes, habits, and culture have been passed on throughout history. Only after the experience of belonging in a safe and supportive family is a child ready for the influence of spiritual, social, and academic communities.

Montessori was not originally an educator, but a medical doctor and anthropologist. In developing her method of supporting the optimum and complete development of human beings she studied education of the past.

Those who do not learn history are doomed to repeat it
—George Santayana, Philosopher

Children in ancient Rome learned at home how to run a farm and be a good person. If they went to school they studied math, Greek, and Latin but the main focus in school was learning how to be an effective speaker. The education of Pre-

Colombian, Inca, and Mayan children emphasized a strong work ethic, character training and being a good community member, and their priests and leaders studied astronomy, architecture, medicine, and the arts. Egyptians emphasized reading and writing and the Greeks included politics and military training. The ancient Chinese taught their children rituals and music, and an education in India included prayers and the subjects of philosophy, law, and morality.

In Montessori we begin with observation and discovery of the human being at all ages of development, and strive to provide a way to bring forth the best. Rather than using an externally-designed educational curriculum, instead we put the human being at the center.

> *Education should no longer be mostly imparting of knowledge, but must take a new path, seeking the release of human potentialities.*
> — Montessori, *Education for a New World.*

Montessori's most valuable discovery occurred early in her work and has been confirmed over and over throughout the years. This discovery was that, given the correct prepared environment, activities that involve the hand and mind working together for an intelligent purpose, and having periods of deep concentration on such work respected and not interrupted, a new kind of human being emerges.

We have learned that it is not necessary to teach a person to work hard, to love learning and acquiring knowledge, to solve problems, be kind and compassionate and help each other, to respect and care for the earth; these characteristics are inborn and natural for the human being when needs have been met.

> *When the children had completed an absorbing bit of work, they appeared rested and deeply pleased. It almost seemed as if a road had opened up within their souls that led to all of their latent powers, revealing the better part of themselves. They exhibited a great affability to everyone, put themselves out to help others and seemed full of good will.*
>
> *It was clear to me that the concept of order and the development of character, of the intellectual and emotional life, must derive from this veiled source. Thereafter, I set out to find experimental objects that would make this concentration possible, and carefully worked out an environment that would present the most favorable external conditions for this concentration.*
>
> *And that is how my method began.*
> — Montessori, *The Child in the Family*

What we think of as traditional education in the West today does not have a long history. The following information is from the book *Montessori, the Science Behind the Genius,* by Dr. Angeline Stoll Lillard, in the chapter "An Answer to the Crisis in Education":

> *The practice of having single-age classrooms began early, apparently in 1847 in Quincy, Massachusetts.*

Another common practice instituted at this time was the . . . practice of shifting children from room to room every 50 minutes at the ring of a bell. This was instigated in the early 1900s. Conventional classrooms today still shift topics not when the teacher and children are at a good transition point, but when the bell rings.

Pre-established schedules restrict the possibility of children's needs guiding the lessons and their timing.

Another drawback is that children can rarely pursue individual interests and activities, but instead have to follow the program that all the children follow, which is predetermined by the teacher or administrators. When it is math time, everyone must do math, no matter how engrossed some might be in a writing project.

The world we are preparing children to work in today is not like this: Educated people often determine for themselves when to move from one piece of work to another. Yet the conventional school system still operates like a factory.

In our current informational age, when we deal in more of a commerce of ideas and entrepreneurship than in factory production, use of such a model in education should be particularly suspect. The school system in a sense trains children to be alike, whereas the economy thrives on variations in individual initiative, at least at the levels to which most parents aspire for their children. The factory model makes poor sense both from the standpoint of how children learn and from the standpoint of what society seeks.

I have met parents sometimes confused and frustrated by their children's response to traditional education—being turned off of learning, working only for grades, and being physically, mentally, and emotionally stressed by the academic and schedule pressure.

I have met many wonderful and dedicated teachers who entered the profession because they love learning and want to share this love with students. They become frustrated when bound by these restrictions.

It is my hope that this book will help all of us look at education for the future in a new way, to follow the interests of individuals and to be inspired by their self-designed paths, and to respect their focus and concentration. I hope this "one family's story" will inspire thinking about how to prepare ourselves to be able to answer our children's needs and their questions about what matters, and to prepare them to meet, with strength, creativity, and wisdom the unforeseen events of the future.

> *The laws governing the universe can be made interesting and wonderful to the child, more interesting even than things in themselves, and he begins to ask: What am I? What is the task of humans in this wonderful universe? Do we merely live here for ourselves, or is there something more for us to do? Why do we struggle and fight? What is good and evil? Where will it all end?*
> —Montessori, *To Educate the Human Potential*

HOW WE BEGAN

When Michael was born his sisters were already teenagers, both of them having experienced Montessori during the primary (age 2.5-6) and elementary (age 6-12) years. So it had been several years since there had been any Montessori-type toys and books in our home. When we went shopping for the new baby we were surprised that these items were difficult to find, having been replaced by plastic and make-believe toys.

Narda and Ursula said to me, "Why don't you start a Montessori toy store?"

I replied, "Why don't you look into it?"

The Michael Olaf Montessori Store, named by the girls after their little brother, Michael Olaf, became a reality. Montessori teachers visiting the San Francisco Bay Area asked if they could order from home so we assembled a list of the products we carried. Then we were asked for pictures so I drew them. The catalogue pages were photocopied and stapled together. Eventually Michael Olaf became a real business, both mail order and storefront.

When Michael was in his third year at the local Montessori school he overheard Jim and me talking about some of the homeschooling families that came into the store. We had noticed that these parents and children often discussed purchases together, considering what they were interested in learning, how much money they had to spend, and what things cost. Something else we noticed was, in most homeschooling families, the respect they had for each other in their conversations, just like one would expect to find between adults and children in Montessori classes. It made sense; when families are together most of the time maybe they learn how to spend time together more politely and more happily.

As we talked more about the thoughtful choices these families were making in order to feed curiosity and follow a child's interest, Michael said he would like to homeschool after he finished the year at the Montessori school.

We were very nervous at the idea because we had not heard much about homeschooling at that point. Originally I had planned to return to teaching 6-12 classes but had become completely involved with helping to run the Michael Olaf Company. So we started researching the legality of homeschooling; we found that California law at that time gave homeschooling families two choices.

The first choice was to register as a private school even if there were only just a few people involved, mother and father as teachers and one or more children as students. However it would be necessary to abide by the laws of private schools, which looked overwhelming, and very un-Montessori to us.

The second choice was to register with a public school, meet with the teacher weekly, and follow the same curriculum that all children in that school district were following. This was also something we were not interested in.

So we homeschooled without doing either, just keeping a record and a notebook of work for each year so we could show that we were doing our best if that ever became necessary. It was these records that I am using to create this book.

Jim and I were a bit worried about beginning this journey so told Michael that we would try it for one year.

After years of teaching children from age two through thirteen in Montessori classes I planned to follow the method I would be using for students in a Montessori class at any age:

1 - Keep the developmental stage in mind.

2 – Prepare the environment and offer the work.

3 - Observe to see if it is working.

4 - Adapt and "Follow the child."

Socialization

This is always the first question anyone asked us over the years, "What about socialization?"

Dr. Angeline Lillard, in her book *Montessori, the Science Behind the Genius* traces the development of what she calls the "factory model" of education where students of the same or similar ages began to be grouped together for efficiency in passing on information, not really to address the needs of children.

We thought a lot about this in beginning our journey. Our own friends were not our age and this is true today. We found that multi-age socialization was one of the most valuable elements in homeschooling.

Just as I had found when teaching 2.5-7 and 6-13 Montessori classes, it was clear that Michael's education, in the broadest sense of the word, was more effective, interesting, and fun because the ages differences were vast. He had older and younger people to learn with, to help and teach, and from whom to be helped and taught. You will read examples of Michael interacting with babies and with very old people, and learning to feel confortable with people of any age.

Concentration

Respecting deep concentration is the number one consideration in Montessori classes and it was for our homeschooling. It had been our parenting guideline from the day Michael was born. We didn't wake him up if he was sleeping, and we looked carefully to see what he was focused on before ever interrupting.

As a result he was used to long periods of concentration. Amusingly, even though he was in a very good Montessori primary class for three years, he often disappeared into his room when he got home in the afternoon, just wanting to be left alone to concentrate on building blocks, drawing, thinking. And as it was Michael's desire to homeschool instead of continuing with his Montessori class we thought perhaps he was asking for more and longer periods of uninterrupted concentration.

As we prepared for this experiment we also thought a lot about our own need for silence and concentration as parents. My own happiest memories throughout childhood were when I was alone and in nature, climbing trees or walking along the river, or in my room reading or listening to music. Jim's good memories were similar.

I do not have nostalgic memories of parties or gatherings of people, in school or socially. At home, whenever we had large family meals (this is a story that was often shared over the years by my mother and we laughed about it), I would excuse myself to go to the bathroom — and not come back! I would go to my room to be alone.

As I look at the activities my husband and I enjoy today in our own non-work time, they are mostly things that we do on our own or quietly together, gardening, playing music, walking, reading, meditating, and so on.

The Environment and Materials

How did we prepare the environment? Already I had had the experience of teaching "Montessori" in a traditionally structured private girls' school in Lima, Peru where I learned that it is very possible, when the teacher is well-trained, to "do Montessori" with no Montessori materials.

That memory gave us courage because we weren't going to be able to rely on Montessori materials, or materials of any kind, because we lived in a very small house in Oakland,

California. The best part of our home was a back deck and fenced garden where Michael was free to be at any time. The classroom was our home, inside and outside, and everywhere else we went in the city and travels elsewhere over the years.

For the first year the educational books and materials we gathered were kept in two small bookcases in the dining room; I would say in total we had 6-8 feet of shelf space. On the shelves there were many books, a supply of paper, and good quality art materials.

However, as much of the homeschooling education was going about daily life together as a family, the "educational materials" were tools and items in the home that we all used to cook, clean, garden, play music, take care of Michael's cat, and entertain guests.

Schedule

There was no 9-3 school-day schedule; schooling was as likely to occur in the evenings and weekends as during the weekdays. In the beginning it was logical that when Jim left for work and I would begin my own full-time work of writing and designing the catalog for our Michael Olaf Montessori company, that Michael concentrated on his own work. But sometimes I worked in the Michael Olaf store, or shopped for groceries, or went on other normal everyday excursions, and Michael went with me.

Curriculum

We did not follow any standard curriculum—not even those standard middle and high school classes that we have been taught are so vital for academic success. Michael did not prepare for any tests until it was time to apply to college.

But even without spending years on "math and language" and other requirements, Michael completed a degree in music at Brown University in three years, went through law school, and now is a musician and, with his wife, the head of their law firm.

Record Keeping

Michael sometimes kept a journal, but only to remember the events of a trip or experience, or to carefully and beautifully, sometimes with decorated margins, record work he wanted to remember and be able to look back on. So these journals are works of art that he is pleased to share today with nephews and nieces.

Once a week I sat down with Michael and together we made a 1-page suggested study schedule that he was in charge of completing at the end of the week. If he didn't get to some of it he added it to the following week's schedule. If he worked on, or completed, projects that were not on the schedule he added them in order to keep track of what he was doing. As I look back it seems clear that these experiments in time-management, that changed through the years, provided excellent preparation for university, and for work, learning, and other goals, throughout life.

An Overview of the Years

Michael ended up homeschooling most of the time through elementary, middle, and high school. Each year, continuing with homeschool or going part time to school, was completely his choice. Over the years he sometimes joined different kinds of alternative education groups, but he always returned to homeschooling because then he was in charge of his own education.

Was I the Perfect Mother/Teacher?

As I look back on this chapter it sounds all so neat and tidy, so logical and perfect. But it was not.

At times Jim and I, trying to be the best parents possible, found ourselves on an emotional roller coaster, sometimes worrying that we were doing the wrong thing and ruining Michael's life; but thank goodness more often we felt that this was the best experience we could be giving our family and Michael.

For the most part I was just as patient and observant and respectful as I always tried to be when in the classroom. But working fulltime in my home office, while homeschooling, required more time and energy, and skill and patience, than being a full-time teacher in a classroom. Here is a note from one of Michael's early journals. I hope he didn't feel this way very often.

Homeschooling Benefits

Thinking back over the years during the process of writing this book we began to understand that these homeschooling years were not just about academics, but about creating a very close, trusting, and loving family, having time to become a good friend and to help others, exploring the meaning of life, becoming creative, and developing the confidence and strength to meet goals and to handle adversity and solve problems.

Michael is a happy, balanced, compassionate, creative human being who loves working hard, making music, taking care of rescued dogs and cats, and contributing to society. He still loves silence and working alone.

We know, from reading about the lives of Montessori school graduates such as the Google creators Larry Page and Sergey Brin, Prince William and Prince Harry of England, Dr. T. Berry Brazelton, Julia Child, Gabriel Garcia Marquez, and many others, and from our own personal experience, that a Montessori education has the potential to allow the fullest development of people who think outside the box, and who follow their instincts and interests in unique and valuable paths.

The Purpose of This Book

In the following chapters of this book we share just a few of the details and pictures of work from each of the years we homeschooled, and some of the books and materials we used. I hope you enjoy traveling through this family journey with us and maybe get some ideas of things to do with your children.

THE GRADES

Ages and Mentors

In dividing Montessori classes into age groupings we usually do not speak of first grade, second grade, third grade, and so on. Rather the method of education is divided into various stages of development: infant community (age 1-2.5), primary (age 2.5-6.5), elementary (age 6-12), middle school (age 12-15), and high school (age 15-18). But for clarity the years in this book will be labeled by grades.

In my own teaching experience the advantages of having as wide an age span as possible—for example elementary students from six to twelve years of age in one class—became clear. The youngest have good social models and are exposed to a high level of academic work; the oldest are able to solidify their own learning, and they become aware of their value as a person, through helping and teaching younger students. In this situation it is quite normal for an older student to return to early work with a new perspective, and for younger students to master work at a level intended for older students. This is just what ideally happens in any vibrant community where everyone benefits from the elders interacting with the youngest and every generation in between.

As an example one year I opened a new elementary class for a school in California. All of the students were between the ages of 5.5 to 7, except for one girl who was 11 years old. Later her mother told me that that was the best year of this girl's whole school experience.

So our plan was to find valuable social situations, inspiring mentors, and ways for Michael to contribute, with no consideration of ages.

Overview of Academic Knowledge

In Montessori classes for children of all ages, all subjects are connected; a child naturally moves from biology to history to art, and so on. However there is a basic structure of knowledge, a division of subjects in order to present a balance.

When I was in university one year I worked in a bookstore and was in charge of tracking and restocking books. I had thought that I was pretty well read at that point, but this work opened my eyes. I realized that when entering any bookstore until then I had usually headed for the same areas and ignored others. Through this experience I learned to appreciate and even develop curiosity for all of the areas of knowledge, non-fiction and fiction. I felt later that this was a good preparation for my becoming a Montessori teacher when I would be doing the same for students.

At the elementary level and beyond, these areas are divided into the "five great lessons" and when entering my own elementary classes it was always clear as one looked around the room that the environment—the timelines, charts, materials, experiments, and books—were divided into these five basic areas. This helps the students, and the teacher, keep a broad overview of knowledge always in mind in guiding exploration and planning work. Here are the areas:

1 – *The Earth.* This includes creation of the universe and the solar system, the beginnings of astronomy, physics, chemistry, physical geography, and geology.

2 – *Plants and Animals.* The adaptation, functions, evolution, and interactions, of plant and animals, botany and zoology.

3 – *People.* The evolution of early humans through ancient and modern civilizations of the world. The focus on the basic physical, mental, and spiritual needs of humans and what we all have in common. Also included are studies of economic geography (exports and imports), migrations, agrarian and other revolutions, and the creations of humans such as music, art, and theatre.

4 – *Language.* Tracing the need for and development of languages, the spread of languages and how they change, grammar, literature, reading and writing, communication of all kinds.

5 – *Math and Geometry.* Beginning with the need for, and development of, both math and geometry through the history of humans; practical and abstract math and geometry used today.

Montessori spent several years developing ways to make math and geometry as exciting and enjoyable for the elementary student as all of the other subjects, but this work had not been translated into English at that time.

We tried to focus on developing the logical mathematical mind in a variety of ways rather than insisting that Michael spend time memorizing and working on elements of math and geometry that were unrelated to life. In his own words he says of this part of his homeschooling experience:

> *Everything I learned in logic I remember, everything I learned in math I forgot.*

When Michael needed math skills for college applications, or at university, or in adult life, he developed them quickly because it was his choice, he knew how to concentrate and work hard, and there was a clear reason for mastery. Then the work was satisfying, enjoyable, and remembered.

Preparation at the Primary Level

Before age six or seven, when a child is at the motor-sensorial stage of development all of these areas are prepared for in such a way that it aids developing control of movement, refinement of the senses, and observation skills. The preparation for the areas of the five great lessons is presented in a practical and sensorial way. All of this primary preparation is covered in my book *The Red Corolla, Montessori Cosmic Education* (for age 3-6+).

Throughout our homeschooling years these five areas were always our guiding structure, much more than any curriculum that might be followed by so many of Michael's friends. Sometimes this caused confusion. For example I remember one day Michael had come home from a friend's house with a question about what he was studying because there were school subjects that his public school friends were studying and talking about that he knew nothing about. He wondered what he was missing.

We pointed out the many subjects that he was interested in at the moment, that he was researching and learning about, such as the Mayan civilization, the lineage of the emperors of Rome, an Indian epic The Mahabharata, the development of politics and checks and balances of government in the United States, and the study of music. He was reassured. So were we.

The Michael Olaf Montessori Shop

At the end of some of the sections in the early chapters of this book you will find a list of a few of the items that were reviewed and selected in that area during that year for the Montessori shop catalog. Michael and his friends reviewed some of them. As the Montessori teacher I had the final say in selection.

The Michael Olaf Company at the time of this writing, 2020, does not carry most of these items. As Jim and I are now in our 70's we are almost retired. We publish my Montessori books and stock them, and we still provide some very special items for ages 0-7 that are difficult to find.

The reason we give the lists of products we used to carry is because we think that these or similar games, toys, tools, and books might be valuable for families at home and some schools. As we all know, even if children are in school all day, their main learning occurs in the home.

KINDERGARTEN

This journey began in June of 1987, when Michael was five and a half years old. We didn't see any reason to wait until fall since he was so excited to begin. One of Montessori's most famous quotes is:

The greatest sign of success for a teacher is to be able to say, The children are now working as if I do not exist.

This sentiment reassured me that working full time from home — being in charge of assessing materials for the Michael Olaf Company and tracking inventory — was going to contribute to my keeping out of Michael's way while he educated himself.

The First Day

I had thought about what I could offer Michael in the basic five academic areas and collaboration in everyday activities of a home. I made a list on a clipboard for this first day to prepare to give suggestions, just as I would have done for each student on the first day of school. On this very special first very exciting morning, I showed him my list.

There was a moment of silence. His face registered several emotions, from surprise to dismay, as he prepared to respond politely, and then he said:

If I had wanted to do all this stuff
I would have stayed in school!

I don't remember what happened next after we both stopped laughing, but in the rest of this chapter I will share some examples, from our written records, of what occurred during this this first experimental year.

Stages of Development

The kindergarten year was a transition between the first, motor-sensorial developmental stage, and the second stage during which a child explores through his imagination, is interested in the big questions that adults ask—justice, fairness, how civilizations evolved, what is the meaning of life—and in working more in groups as a way to explore the function of society. So it took observation and experimentation to bridge the gap.

Social Life and Alone Time, Striking a Balance

Having time together as a family became so much more relaxed and enjoyable which was a happy discovery as we began to homeschool. Jim left each week-day morning for work as a painter for the Berkeley schools and I was in charge of tracking inventory, ordering, and testing products to carry in the Michael Olaf Company, sometimes working in the store and other times working with our employees.

So, although I was there for Michael if he needed me, and we often enjoyed spending time together on a project, our main time together consisted of weekly discussions of what might be good to explore and what skills to work on for the following week.

A few years later I was interviewed on the radio along with another mother with two daughters homeschooling. The interviewer asked, "How much time do you think you spend each week sitting down with your homeschoolers and actually teaching?"

Simultaneously we both replied, "About two hours."

She leaned forward with her mouth open, surprised into silence. It is not what people expect to hear, but it held true throughout the years. Jim and I helped Michael think about learning, and gave suggestions, but Michael was in charge of his time and his learning.

In my Montessori 6-12 classes, at the beginning of each year I gave the five great lessons to the new children but usually older children came as well and shared the depth of their learning that had began with these lessons.

I gave the follow-up lessons to one student at a time, depending on an interest expressed by that child, because I did not want to interrupt the work and deep concentration of the other students. Students kept records of who had had which lessons, and they taught the follow-up lessons to each other.

If a teacher had to teach each follow-up lesson, for each area, to each child, we would have the kind of schedule that we avoid in Montessori, children waiting to be told what to be doing next all day, instead of having days and weeks of time to manage themselves.

Having already tasted the joy of uninterrupted concentration and of having his "work" choice and schedule respected, Michael was very good at keeping himself happily occupied all day. In the evenings and on weekends Michael often spent time with his older sisters, and as we were very close to two families in the neighborhood, with these friends. He also took art classes in the neighborhood, sometimes with one of his best friends from the Montessori school.

A large part of my own store work was to send for games, books, and other educational materials that might be appropriate for schools or families interested in Montessori kinds of educational materials for homes and schools. Because our family were together most of each day of the week there was a spirit of working together and helping each other so it was natural for Michael, and his friends in the neighborhood, to be involved with the testing, reading, and research of toys, games, and books.

Academics

We always kept in mind these five areas: the earth, plants and animals, humans, language and math. At first I offered the lessons in these areas that are offered in the primary class, as presented in the book *The Red Corolla, Montessori Cosmic Education* (for age 3-6+). However many of the lessons and activities in this book are interesting and valuable for both primary and elementary students. At that time Michael was moving toward interest in more imaginative, less sensorial, exploration and in combining interests in two or more areas at the same time. This is typical of the child from 6-12.

In the following pages you will see some of the work Michael did this year and also some of the educational materials that were deemed of value to be included in our catalog.

THE EARTH

Simple physics experiments to explore sound, water, heat, electricity, and other physical science principles, were casually carried out. For example, sometimes we found ourselves exploring the work of wind and water at the beach, or exploring in ways that were similar to the primary experiments such as "Candle in Limited Air" at the dinner table. These were not formal lessons but activities that could for the most part be explored with objects found in the home or in nature.

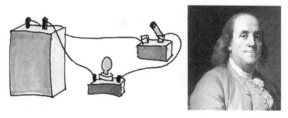

The picture above shows a simple electric circuit that we later had made to sell at the Michael Olaf Company because it was impossible to find anything simple, clear, and well made commercially available. Such simple experiments as this one lay a firm sensorial foundation for the work in the elementary class. At age 6-12+ the study in this area feeds an ever-broadening understanding of the sciences and principles at work in the creation of the universe, the solar system, and the earth.

On our weekly visits to the local library we looked for age appropriate physical science books and biographies of scientists, explorers, archaeologists, and geologists.

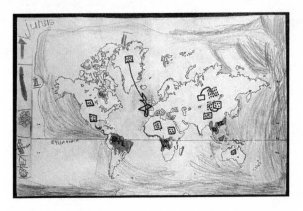

We found some outline maps of the world and, along with a colored globe Michael could create his own depiction of where in the world there are jungles, deserts, cold lands, mountains and Mediterranean climate. This was the start of an interest in why people live the way they do because of the environment. How did they dress? What did they eat? What were their homes like? How did they travel and defend themselves? So it was obvious that the elementary mind of imagination was beginning to function, connecting all subjects.

Michael Olaf Company Selections

Here are some of the items that Michael and his friends and Jim and I tested and selected for the Michael Olaf Company catalog for this year in this area: rock collection, gem and mineral card game, sun print kit, prism, planet mobile, electric circuit card game, globes, puzzle maps, flags, books on scientists, physics experiments, and the physical world

PLANTS AND ANIMALS

For botany we did many of the experiments that I used in my primary classes. One example explores the needs of the plant for light, heat, and water. We planted seeds in several containers, checked them once a week, and Michael drew pictures of what was happening. One container received no light, another received no water, another was provided no heat (it was kept in the refrigerator) and one received everything: light, water, and heat. Above is his record (my writing and his drawing) of the final week.

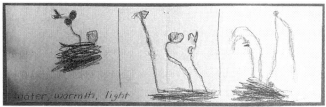

water, warmth, light

We spent a lot of time outside, in our small back yard where we had a small garden, and in the neighborhood. Just as Montessori once pointed out to teachers who had complained about the difficulty of exploring nature in cities, there was a lot to discover; we found plants peeking up between the cracks in the sidewalks, birds nesting in our own trees, and so much more.

Coming home from a nature walk Michael sometimes recorded, with pictures and writing, his memories or what was most important to him. He did not keep these records in a journal but in a folder, sometimes making books held together by punching holes in the edge and fastening them with little plastic loops or yarn.

You can see throughout the kindergarten pages that at this point Michael's writing was not as beautiful as he would have liked so, never mentioning the fact, I always gave him the choice, "Do you want me to write and you draw or do you want to do the writing too?"

Then, just as in the primary class, I would write slowly, carefully, and neatly in front of him, because the adult is the model for writing just as for everything else.

Above is a report from a visit to a local park. He saw "birds and one dead fish" (asking that I do the writing) and gathered leaves to press.

We often studied the shapes of leaves and other elements of botany in the beginning, because this was one of my interests as a child and as a Montessori teacher, but it was clear that Michael was more interested in animals than in plants. He was very attentive to his cat that had come to us as a kitten, and was so fascinated with the American buffaloes that for his seventh birthday he planned a party that consisted of taking his friends from Oakland across the bridge to see the buffalo in Golden Gate Park in San Francisco, and then back across the bridge to see the buffalo in the Oakland zoo. His interest in, and care for, animals was as true throughout the homeschooling years as it is today.

Just as in a Montessori class we never pushed him in any direction. I continued to offer botany elements, along with everything else, each year, but then withdrew and watched to see which direction he would take guided by his own curiosity.

If a person were required to study everything equally there would be no chance to delve deeply into anything. The possibility to choose one path over another and to have this choice respected is one of the best things about a Montessori education.

An interesting piece of work, freely chosen, which has the virtue of inducing concentration rather than fatigue, adds to the child's energies and mental capacities, and leads {the child} to self-mastery.
— Montessori, *The Absorbent Mind*

Michael Olaf Company Selections

Here are some of the items that we approved for inclusion in the Michael Olaf Company plant and animal section of our catalog in the kindergarten year: plant/animal classification cards, dinosaur models, fossil collection, a butterfly garden, bird song recordings and books, card games to learn about plants and animals, a shell collection and matching cards, and cards that classified vertebrate animals into classes: fish, amphibians, reptiles, birds, and mammals

PEOPLE

Humans throughout history and all over the world want the same things for themselves and their families. This emphasis on common human needs, on how we are all alike at this level, is presented in Montessori social studies at every level.

This area is first introduced in the early years through the senses, with real experiences of the food, music, dance, art, and traditions of people around the world. Then we start to learn the details, the eventual goal being the realization that people throughout history have met the physical needs of food, housing, clothing, and transportation because of their physical environment.

We were lucky to live in a place where there exists a diverse cultural heritage. Michael's best friend in his Montessori primary class was from Ethiopia. Each year we went to the celebration of the Swedish Christmas with a Santa Lucia festival of lights, Swedish dance, food, and clothing. The museums in the San Francisco Bay area provided an excellent introduction to many cultures. And at our library visits we looked for books about the various cultures of the world.

The picture above shows a book on Greece that Michael created. I don't know what inspired his interest in this country but he made a flag of the country with strips of white and blue paper, and drew a picture of Greece for the front of the book.

When children are encouraged to look at a globe or map and draw their own countries rather than tracing outlines, they look carefully at the borders as they draw and much more information is stored in the brain. Even I have a better sense of the shape of this country after seeing his drawing.

Old copies of the magazine National Geographic were easy to obtain when I was a teacher and during our homeschooling years. Michael would look for the country of interest, in this case Greece, and find pictures related to food, shelter, transportation, and clothing, then cut them out and paste them to the pages of his book. This process reinforces the fact that all humans are the same in many ways, and that our own culture is just one of many.

Music

The mother in one of the two close families in our neighborhood, Geri Walther, was a violist in the San Francisco symphony. Michael was used to hearing her practice when visiting their home. Occasionally she would take Michael, her daughter Argenta, and me to afternoon rehearsals with her. Davies Hall was empty except for the musicians on the stage and we had the Presidents Box (the best way to observe) all to ourselves. I took paper and crayons along and time was divided between watching the musicians, listening to the directions of the conductor, listening to some of the most beautiful music in the world, lying on the floor drawing and coloring, and occasionally going out into the hall (out of earshot of the musicians) and running up and down on the carpet.

Art

Almost everything we studied was connected with art. The observation skills, the personal expression, the pencil grip used in drawing, the eye-hand control, all are valuable, and even help prepare for beautiful writing.

I never used adult-created outlines to be colored in when teaching and we didn't have coloring books at home. When an adult creates the drawing this gives a child a message that his own attempts aren't good enough. Yet many great artists have tried, are trying, to create just the kinds of original drawings that children create spontaneously and naturally.

On the left side of the picture above, you can see a page from a book of intricate designs to be copied. On the right is a drawing by Michael that combines several things he must have been thinking about at the time.

Classes

There was a local arts center where Michael attended classes with Mikael, his Ethiopian friend from the Montessori school. They went together on the weekend to study weaving, clay, drawing, and painting.

For a short time Michael took piano and violin lessons but we found out early that, just like people can use the name "Montessori" without really being trained to teach authentic Montessori, the same is true for Suzuki music lessons so this didn't last long. Instead Jim and I just shared what we knew on piano and guitar.

Michael Olaf Company Selections

Here are some of the items that were tested by us and chosen to be included in the Michael Olaf Company catalog for this year in learning about humans: books about early humans, ancient civilizations, and the physical needs of cultures around the world, past and present. Books and playing cards about famous people including scientists, political figures, artists and so on. A game called *About American History. California Bingo* game. A workbook for tracing one's own family tree. Cooperative, non-competitive games of all kinds that emphasize working together and helping each other rather than competing and winning

LANGUAGE

Literature - Family Readings

From the time Michael was very young, just as with his older sisters, it was a tradition to read books aloud as a family before bed. It was such a pleasurable experience that years later, when Michael came home at Christmas vacation during his first year at university this is what he wanted to do.

Adults are always the best models, the best teachers for a child's language. But so is great literature. Reading aloud is how we introduced the writings that open the mind to different ways of thinking, and introduce subjects that wouldn't come up in daily conversation. This increased our whole family's vocabulary and understanding of concepts and inspired interesting conversations.

Later, as Michael was able to read well we would often start a book one evening and then be too busy for Jim or me to read the next day. Michael would get tired of waiting for us and he would continue the book on his own. This became a way for us to inspire him to read books on his own that he might not have tackled otherwise. We all knew it was a "trick."

Verbal Expression

We also emphasized expressive recitation during these family readings instead of reading the words in a monotone, so that the emotions, the suspense, drama, and the humor, could be heard in the reading.

This is the way a teacher reads in order to keep the attention of children, but children also enjoy learning to read this way. Then reports given in class are not just monotone readings, but interesting to the audience. Both Jim and Michael, natural mimics, were very skilled at this.

During the day sometimes Michael would draw or write important memories from these readings. Below you see what he illustrated and wrote, part of the poem "The Crocodile" by Lewis Carroll:

How doth the little crocodile improve his shining tail
then welcome little fishes in with gently smiling jaws.

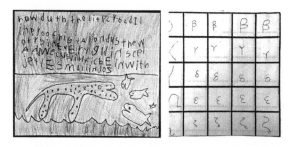

Next to the crocodile writing you can see Michael's attempt at copying Greek letters. This is a page from his book on Greece.

Writing and Handwriting

Handwriting does not improve by just repeating the same "ugly" letters over and over and hoping for the best, but by practicing the skills necessary for writing in a way one can be proud of.

Authentic Suzuki music instruction divides a piece of music (such as *Twinkle, Twinkle, Little Star*) into tiny increments, each providing a challenge that matches the child's potential ability in the moment. This supports the continually advancing skills (placement of the feet, posture, position of arms, hands, and fingers) necessary for playing beautiful music from the very beginning. A child is provided with experiences of success, which inspires more work, which results in more success, then more work, and on and on.

We found this process an example of how to think of learning in any area of knowledge.

Michael was slowly working on improving his cursive handwriting. But as it was not as good as he would have liked

I never required that he write so he would often dictate the words to me if there was something he wanted to record.

Many years ago, when I had a primary student who entered the class at age 4.5, too old to be interested in learning the shapes and sounds by means of the sandpaper letters, I designed a new activity called "rainbow letters". The materials were a tray, ¼ page pieces of white paper, and a cup for gathering a selection of colored pencils. Very, very carefully I would write the letter in front of him and then show him how to trace close to the line with a second color, creating the beginning of a rainbow.

In the Montessori class the sandpaper letters could be used to get started, but I have shown this activity to many teachers over the years and it has been very successful for children who are past the age of being interested in sandpaper letters. Quite often the children will go on to make books with covers decorated with their self-chosen "best" sandpaper letters. The picture above is of one of our grandchildren enjoying this work in our home.

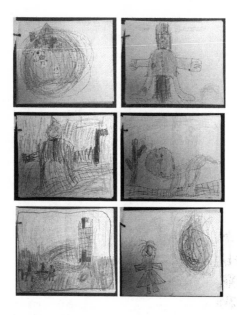

As Michael was casually improving his writing of letters, he sometimes chose to express his thoughts with only pictures, and sometimes with pictures and sentences. Above are six pages from a 19-page book, with cover, that he "wrote" after we read the book and saw the movie of "The Wizard of Oz". See if you can recognize some of the characters and events of this story.

Errors in Writing

Making errors is just part of the learning process. As in my classrooms we did not use erasers. Errors in writing were just lightly crossed out and Michael would go on writing. This helped him focus on getting the words, the ideas, down on paper without being interrupted. Learning to make corrections comes later.

Spelling

Writing and spelling are two completely different skills. We never referred to his beginning attempts at spelling as anything but his own personal creations. He would gradually become aware of correct spelling through my writing for him and his reading.

We followed the maxim, *Teach by teaching, not by correcting.*

Reading

Here is a list Michael dictated to me, "Books I Read in Kindergarten". The first few were early readers the titles of which wouldn't mean anything so I will leave those out. The rest were either *Ladybird* books from the UK, or children's books with lovely pictures and a few sentences per page. We focused on non-fiction books and traditional stories that have stood the test of time for being interesting and valuable. Most of the books were brought home from our weekly trip to the library.

Here are the titles:

The Lion, The Robin, The Monkey, The Tiger, The Three Little Pigs (many more non-fiction books about individual animals, farms, jungle animals, pets, etc.), *The Ugly Duckling, Peter and the Wolf, Puss in Boots, Thumbelina, The Elves and the Shoemaker, Billy Goats Gruff, Hansel and Gretel, Sleeping Beauty, The Pied Piper of Hamelin, Jack and the Beanstalk, Pinocchio.* Also these titles: *The Many Lives of Benjamin Franklin, A Little Schubert, Fossils Tell of Long Ago,* and *Evolution*

Grammar

It is only natural when a child is focusing carefully on the written word and in learning to write sentences, that he wants to discuss and learn about grammar.

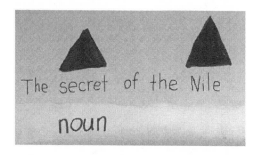

Michael had been introduced to the differences between parts of speech such as nouns, verbs, adjectives, etc., in his primary class so we continued this work. We didn't have any of the materials so he would pick out a sentence that he liked, I would write it, and he would draw the symbol with felt pens. An example is above.

Since he was approaching the 6-12 stage of development and interested in ancient civilizations, I could explain that the

43

large black triangle that represented the noun stood for the pyramids in Egypt, and the red circle that represented the verb for a bouncing ball, always in motion. I made up sentences that were connected to our life or his interests and he would identify nouns, verbs, conjunctions, and other parts of speech.

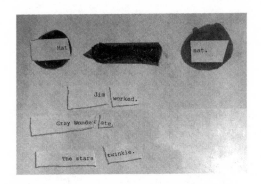

It was the same with analyzing sentences. Michael had already started to learn about the parts of a sentence in the primary class so we continued this.

In a Montessori primary class there would be a folder of prepared slips for a student to cut up and place on the wooden symbols. So I typed up sentences having to do with our life for him to cut up. In this case, for example: Mat sat (from an early reading book he had discovered): Jim (his dad) worked; Gray Wonder (his cat) ate; The stars twinkle.

Then he would draw and color in the symbol as in the picture above. A black circle for the subject of the sentence, a red circle for the predicate or verb, and a black arrow showing that the activity was carried out by the subject.

Michael Olaf Company Selections

Here are some of the items that were included in the Michael Olaf Company catalog for this year having to do with learning language: picture vocabulary books, foreign language tapes of simple sentences and songs, poetry books, "Ladybird" readers from English, abridged classic stories, a simple book with spelling rules, wipe-off plastic writing sheets, a picture *Book of Kells*, a game about myths and legends of different traditions

MATH AND GEOMETRY

Primary Class Sensorial Math and Geometry

In his time in the local Montessori primary class Michael had received a very enjoyable sensorial introduction to these areas through the traditional Montessori materials that one sees all over the world. This math set includes wood and bead materials that introduce, beginning around age 4.5, counting through 1,000; the operations of addition, subtraction, multiplication and division both with simple numbers and the decimal systems with beaded squares and cubes; and fractions. The geometry materials explore plane and three-dimensional geometric figures.

Elementary Class Math and Geometry

At this level math is first introduced through a historical perspective. Why and how did math evolve? Why and how did geometry evolve? This is interesting to all children, but standard math texts that are required in schools around the world usually do not explore these interesting origins of math and geometry.

There are also sensorial materials at this age leading to abstracting the principles and being able to work in one's head instead of with one's hands.

In my experience in the elementary years some children loved math and geometry, perhaps because of the attractive materials and because of my enthusiasm for these subjects, but some did not. I learned that requiring children to work on math, just as requiring them to work on anything else in the elementary curriculum, is sure to discourage them. It is better for them to see that everything is being enjoyed by someone else in the classroom.

For Michael we purchased "Mortenson Math," a set of plastic bars and cubes and booklets that had been developed by a Montessori elementary teacher. This visually, in a Montessori way, explored the basics of areas mentioned above, plus algebra, geometry, fractions, and differential calculus.

The pieces were interesting to explore as they connected Michael to what he had done in math in his Montessori experience, and the booklets were a transition from objects to representation on paper, which was valuable. But over the next few years, filling in the pages of the booklets became as boring, as unrelated to real life, as the repetition math worksheets used in many kinds of schools all over the world.

As a result, beginning in the kindergarten year, we required the minimum of this kind of math, even though this was one area on the California requirements list that we had planned to pay attention to. This work was not Michael's choice, and as he looks back on his education he says this was one area that he didn't enjoy, felt that it was a waste of his time, and he doesn't remember what he learned.

Practical Math

It is more important for students to understand *why* they must study math, and telling them, "It will be useful some day," isn't enough to justify the required hours, days, weeks, years on the subjects. So we found ways to make using the mathematical brain part of everyday life. You will see examples throughout this book. As an example here is a bar graph we created together.

Ages from 0-50 are written along the left-hand vertical line. The members of the family—Jim, Susan, Narda, Ursula, Gray Wonder the cat, and Michael— are listed on the bottom horizontal line. Michael found out the ages of everyone and plotted the bars. This project was connected to everyday life, it was interesting to all, and it worked.

The need to tell time, keep track of dates, and money, were just part of our everyday life so these things were learned without "lessons."

Michael Olaf Company Selections

Here are some of the items that we reviewed and that were included in the Michael Olaf Company catalog for this year in learning about math and geometry: a counting frame, Cuisenaire rods, a math-dice game, a flowchart game, a Ladybird book on world currencies, world times, early number systems, times tables, the Beaufort wind scale and other number-related subjects

FIRST GRADE

Here is a quote from Montessori that we found very helpful in continuing to homeschool:

An inner change has taken place, but nature is quite logical in arousing now in the child not only a hunger for knowledge and understanding, but a claim to mental independence, a desire to distinguish good from evil by [the child's] *own powers, and to resent limitation by arbitrary authority. In the field of morality, the child now stands in need of their own inner light.*

... we have learned from [the child] *certain fundamental principles of psychology. One is that the child must learn by their own individual activity, being given a mental freedom to take what is needed, and not to be questioned in choice. Our teaching must only answer the mental needs of the child, never dictate them. Just as a small child cannot be still because* [the child] *is in need of coordinating movements, so the older child, who may seem troublesome in . . . curiosity over the why, what and wherefore of everything seen, is building up* [the child's] *mind by this mental activity, and must be given a wide field of culture on which to feed.*

The task of teaching becomes easy, since we do not need to choose what we shall teach, but should place all before [the child] *for the satisfaction of . . . mental appetite.* [The child] *must have absolute freedom of choice, and then requires nothing but repeated experiences*

which will become increasingly marked by interest and
serious attention, during his acquisition of some desired
knowledge

> – Montessori,
>
> *To Educate the Human Potential*

The Michael Olaf Company was now supporting us. We didn't want to be a large business, just to be a valuable business, and to return to the countryside after many years of living in cities. Several times we had visited Humboldt County, where Jim had studied acting and mime at Comedia del Arte and The College of the Redwoods. This was a place where the Redwood trees meet the Pacific Ocean, an area famous for nature lovers, artists, musicians, with an airport and a university.

But then a good friend who was teaching a 6-12 class in Marin County visited and saw what Michael was doing and said she would like him to join her class. She kindly offered to drive him to school from Oakland each day. Michael decided to do this. I took turns after school with another East Bay family to pick up the children and drive them home.

So Michael homeschooled for the summer and first semester of first grade and then attended the Montessori elementary class in the spring. It was a great experience; he made new friends and continued the kind of work that he had done in the Montessori primary class in Oakland. However, he missed being able to be outside at any time during the day, deciding his own choices of work, and having long periods of uninterrupted concentration. He wanted to return to homeschooling so we decided to go on with our plans to move to the country after the first grade school year ended.

To Draw or to Write?

You can see in this picture that Michael's penmanship was not good at all, but this was never mentioned. He continued to express what he was learning in the academic areas through art and, as a separate endeavor, learning to develop beautiful handwriting in interesting ways: the rainbow letters with colored pencils, practicing the writing of other languages and cultures, using colored inks with Italic pen points to make wide and narrow strokes, and writing a few letters and then studying them carefully to see what makes a letter beautiful. Is it the width of the loop? What about the slope? When I wrote for him I did so slowly and as perfectly as I could, and made it clear that I enjoyed writing.

Learning handwriting this careful and methodical way is very important because each time a child writes something, the way he constructs the letters — even if they are half in print and half in cursive and some of the letters backwards – this information is stored in the brain as the "correct" way to write.

When a child has learned to write badly in this way it is very difficult to unlearn, so it is far better to have a child express ideas by through drawing and painting while working on penmanship.

In my Montessori classes I had NEVER required children to write until I had helped them learn how to write in such a way that they could be proud of their efforts.

Social Life

In the beginning of the year Ursula was studying at The College of the Arts in Oakland so she and Michael spent a lot of time together, but Narda had moved to Milwaukee, Wisconsin to take the AMI elementary Montessori course. In the second part of the year Ursula studied in Southern California and Michael missed both of his sisters very much. It was very good that this was the semester he was at Marin Montessori School.

Michael still spent a lot of time with close friends in the neighborhood. On the weekends there were swimming classes at the Temescal pool in Oakland where Michael made more friends and learned to swim through several levels of the Red Cross swimming classes.

One of Michael's friends from the Montessori elementary class sometimes came over on weekends and worked on Michael's homeschooling projects with him, such as the Egypt book pictured on the next page.

Service

Caring for others and the environment is part of a Montessori education, at any age. Even in the primary classes when a child finishes an activity such as polishing shoes, everything is put back on the tray, the materials complete, clean, and in order, ready for a friend to use. This consideration for the person who will use the material next is one of the first social acts.

At the elementary age, when one is interested in fairness and how society works best, more thought goes into finding ways to help others. We had heard about a San Francisco Bay Area program called The Co-Workers of Mother Teresa in America that had a program in Oakland on Martin Luther King Jr. Way, not far from us. Michael already knew about Mother Teresa so we asked how we could help. They served a hot lunch daily to AIDS patients and their caregivers, so we found out what they needed, bought the food, and twice a month took it to the center.

Good manners are another element of service as consideration for others. We reviewed a children's manners book for the Michael Olaf company and it was one of our

53

favorites because it was similar to the way these things are taught in a Montessori class: role-playing different situations to practice being considerate and nice in a specific situation instead of embarrassing children by correcting them in front of others.

Academics

We continued to keep in mind the areas of Earth, Plants and Animals, Humans, Language, and Math that you will find on the next pages.

THE EARTH

Although we continued to casually present the physical science experiments mentioned in the last chapter, and learn about the constellations, the visits we took through Northern California this year as we were deciding whether or not to move provided so much more. We drove over mountains and along the coast, stopping to climb rocks and, after we arrived in Humboldt County, visited Fern Canyon which seemed right out of prehistory, and saw lagoons with herds of elk roaming freely. The constellations and everything in the evening, night, and early morning sky was much clearer in this area and the sunsets already brought us to the beaches to see them.

The value of learning about the earth first hand reminded me of an article I had read years ago by a professor at the Massachusetts Institute of Technology. He was bemoaning the fact that incoming students had learned physics from books and computers and had no real experience of the physical world. He said that the students who came directly from life and work on a farm were more prepared for the sciences than those who had learned on a computer. He went on to say that all they need to know of computers could be learned in the first semester.

It is sad that we start children on computers at such an early age these days and perhaps this perspective will help turn this around.

Michael Olaf Company Selections

Here are some of the items that Michael and his friends and parents text and selected for the Michael Olaf Company catalog for this year in this area: Magnet, magnifying glass, *The Big Bang* (written by a Montessori teacher), *Find the Constellations* book, *Glow in the Night Sky* book, solar system mobile, glow stars to create constellations on a ceiling, science experiment books, the ocean and continent puzzle map, Golden Nature Guides to identify stars, and rocks and minerals, and neighborhood geology, the Dymaxion Puzzle Map

PLANTS AND ANIMALS

The Timeline of Life

On walks around the neighborhood we collected leaves, pressed them, and used them in making birthday cards or books such as the one shown here.

But the elementary child is far more interested in *why* leaves are shaped the way they are than in learning the names of the shapes. They want to know which leaves and flowers evolved together and why. So the little classification keys that we carried at the Michael Olaf store were the most helpful. We could pick a leaf from a weed sticking up through the pavement, or a flower in the garden, and in a few minutes, through careful observation and deduction, find out where it is in the grand scheme of botany.

But Michael's real love was animals.

One of the first lessons in the Montessori elementary class is called the Evolution Timeline, or the Timeline of Life. This is a long strip of paper that shows the periods and eras from the time that life first appeared on Earth to the present. The last very small section shows how long modern humans have been on earth. This puts humans in a historical perspective.

Because we did not have the Montessori evolution of life timeline and material, these ideas were introduced through books and small posters of timelines from the Science Academy Museum in San Francisco. Michael decided to remember these stages by drawing his favorite animals during the evolutionary periods, creating his own timeline.

Caring for Animals

The most important lessons in the field of zoology are first-hand experiences getting to know, and learning how to care for, animals. This will lay the foundation for caring for all life on earth as a person grows up. We had friends who owned Llamas and we visited them, fed them, learned about where they came from, and listened to their strange electronic-sounding calls to each other over the hills.

Usually I would stress observing animals in their natural habitat but this was difficult living in a city so we went to zoos. Michael had a cat, a hermit crab, and a guinea pig that he cared for and loved. The guinea pig was chosen for the family Christmas card that year.

The left side of the picture above shows a letter Michael wrote to his friends. One day when he was visiting Sadie and Stefan, a moth landed on Sadie's leg. She yelled and her father instinctively reached out and smashed it. Michael was horrified and immediately stomped home and asked me to write a letter to Sadie and her younger brother.

This is what it said:

Dear Sadie & Stefan, This is the moth speaking. Gray is my favorite color. That is why we moths are gray. Don't kill us or we'll take a message to somebody that doesn't have a home. If you don't do this the person who doesn't have a home will never come to your house and neither will we. You can't visit us. The end

(The reference to "person who doesn't have a home" was Michael. When asked why he said that he replied that his friends all owned their homes and we were renting ours.)

Michael's allowance was not money earned for work that he did as a member of the family but it was considered a share of the family income and he learned early that everyone used their money to contribute to the family expenses; it was not just for toys.

He found a way to help animals with some of his income by adopting, or protecting, a wolf named Tahoma who was born, and is sheltered, at Wolf Haven America, a non-profit in Washington State. This was a project to educate the public about the role of wolves in nature.

Animal Classification

Another piece of Montessori material for the 6-12 class teaches how plants and animals are connected to each other, how they share characteristics and traits. This work evolves naturally from the Evolution Timeline. In class we would study both the "Kingdom Plantae" and the "Kingdom Animalia" and the ancient life forms that belonged to both.

Above you can see the first page of Michael's timeline notebook. Michael and I created it for classifying the Kingdom Animalia including these early phyla through the vertebrates.

Each phylum was labeled and protected by a plastic sheet cover. Michael would search for pictures in nature magazines, and make his own drawings and put them in the pocket in the front of the notebook, and at times sit down and classify them and insert them, sometimes along with text, in the proper section of the book.

As an example he classified his grandparents' golden retriever as: *Kingdom*: Animalia; *Phylum*: Chordate; *Class*: Mammalia; *Order*: Carnivora. Einstein who was one of Michael's favorite historical figures because of a children's book he liked, was similarly classified.

This also is where Michael kept his zoology writing, pictures, and newsletters keeping up-to-date with the wolf Tahoma, and the pictures from his seventh birthday party when he and his friends visited the American buffalo in the Bay Area.

Although it was meant just as an introduction, this homemade timeline book was used for many years. It provided a personal, and a real life understanding of the Linnaeus classification system and more.

Michael Olaf Company Selections

Here are some of the items that we approved and added to the Michael Olaf Company plant and animal section of our catalog this year: a favorite book that was written by a grown-up Montessori student, *Life Story*, presenting the Timeline of life to children, including the Paleozoic, Mesozoic, Cenozoic Eras.

A black and white prehistory timeline; *The Big Bang*; large insect and bird pictures; Cooperative games *Harvest Time, Beautiful Place, Deep Sea Diver, Explorers*, and *Together*; the games *Predator* and *Pollination*; vocabulary cards vertebrate/invertebrate, animals of seven continents, classification of invertebrates; animal models and matching cards for farm and zoo animals; *Flower Finder* and *Tree Finder* classification books; animal books about seeds, *butterfly to caterpillar, chicken to egg*, and *tadpole to frog*; other plant and animal books

PEOPLE

Early Humans

One of the main lessons given at the beginning of each year in the 6-12 class begins with the story of early humans. The last tiny strip of the Evolution Timeline, which shows the amount of time there have been humans on earth relative to all of life, was expanded to create an Early Humans timeline.

Culture and Ninja Turtles

The next aspect of this area has to do with the establishment of cultures beginning with ancient cultures. The study of heroes and villains and their roles in history, is very much of interest at this age. The Ninja Turtles of modern culture arose to meet this interest, as it was something Michael could share with any of his friends from the neighborhood, in art classes, playgrounds, anywhere.

My first introduction to this phenomenon was at a playground when Michael was a baby. A group of young boys and girls were acting out a story, roleplaying characters called Leonardo, Michelangelo, Raphael, and Donatello, four renaissance artists. I thought these young people must surely be students at a local art school until I found out that these were the names of the heroes in the comic books and TV series *Teenage Mutant Ninja Turtles*. Action figures had been created to represent all of the characters and the good turtles, through "Turtle Power," struggled against evil.

We didn't have guns, or action figures in our home so Michael would watch the shows and play with the action figures at the homes of his friends. Then he would come home and create his own action figures with cardboard, paper, tape, glue, string, and felt pens. Above you can see the beginning of his collection laid out on a table.

When a friend and fellow Montessori 6-12 teacher visited one day, she was very impressed and asked Michael if he would be interested in creating figures based on the Greek or Roman Gods. He explained to her that he was not interested; he was exploring heroes and myths in his own way.

To begin to learn about ancient cultures in a traditional classroom a teacher might make an assignment such as, "Let's pick a culture and study it together" or, "Everyone pick a culture and we will each study the culture we have selected."

But in a Montessori elementary class the teacher is constantly observing each child, looking for clues to what the child is interested in at the moment, and then offering suggestions to carry an interest further.

At any one time one child might be following an interest in algebra, another researching an historical event, another working on penmanship, and so on. This respect for individual choice is one of the wonderful elements of Montessori; even though each child will not cover each subject, as they follow their own inner guide, they will be seeing that all avenues of study can be enjoyable and exciting.

Perhaps it was in one of the history books Michael was looking through as we reviewed them for the catalog, but somehow he became interested in ancient Egypt. Especially in the long period of time that the culture spanned and the art and writing with hieroglyphs, from left to right, and then right to left, just as an ox would walk back and forth to plow a field. He became so fascinated in the purposes and construction of the pyramids in Egypt that he asked if we could go there.

Looking at the globe it became clear that that this kind of travel was out of the question, but I explained that there were other pyramid cultures much closer to home, such as the Maya cultures in Mexico. We looked through the newspaper to see what tours would cost, not really thinking that it would be possible, as we didn't travel unless it was to see family or a work conference.

We excitedly discovered that during the spring equinox at Chichen Itza in the Yucatan, on the north stairway of the Castillo de Chichen Itza, a solar projection of a snake of light appears, formed by the shadow cast on the stairs of the pyramid as the sun rises, and people come from all over the world to see this event called "The Serpent of Light.

This meant that, since most people wanted to witness this event, there were few tourists in Chichen Itza during the previous week. We were able to get an inexpensive 4-day tour flying directly to Merida from San Francisco and had the pyramid practically all to ourselves. We were able to experience both an ancient and modern culture, the sights, sounds, traditions, homes, clothing, first hand. This began a years long interest in the Mayan culture for Michael.

Civilization Study Charts

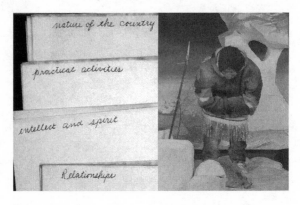

When we returned I offered Michael an adaptation of material I had used in my elementary classes. This material was the Culture Study Charts. I didn't have the charts so I made up cards that could be used instead.

One year, teaching in Marin County California, I took my class to the Museum of the American Indian. Upon returning to the school one of the students decided to use the charts to study the local Miwok Indigenous people's group. He found this so satisfying that when that was finished he went on to study several more Indigenous groups from all over the country. He didn't give any kind of a report or presentation to the class, but all of the other children periodically checked in with his project as he worked on it. They asked questions and were gratified by hearing his answers so they learned a lot even though it wasn't their work.

After our exposure to the Mayan culture, visits to the Hall of Man at the museum in San Francisco became much more real. For example in the picture above an Inuit fisherman is giving a prayer of thanks to the seal he has just caught, believing that the spirit of the seal continually enters seal after seal in order to feed the man's family. This is an example of a belief that would be discovered in researching with the civilization cards.

I will share with you the information on these cards, as this might be interesting in guiding an interest in learning more about any culture. The category (Nature of the Country, Practical Activities, Intellect and Spirit, and Relationships) appears on one side of the card. There are several cards in each category with research questions on the back of each. A student could just choose one card at random, or go through all of the cards and questions and decide where to start, and research only those elements of particular interest.

Nature of the Country: (1) What were the soil and climate like? (2) What flora and fauna existed? (3) What people lived there? (4) Where did the people come from and why?

Practical Activities: (1) How did they find their country and make it habitable? (2) How did they use the natural resources? (3) What were the types of work occupations, products?

Intellect and Spirit: (1) What language? (2) What were the ideas of life and death? Who was the spiritual leader? Justice? (3) What was education like? How advanced was learning? (4) What was art like?

Relationships: (1) What about dress, food, houses, customs, family life, children, government? (2) Were goods held individually or as a group? Did they take care of the poor? (3)

What about travel and migration? Why did groups settle where they did? (4) Trade among selves and with others? How? Barter? (5) Any wars and conquests? Did they make slaves?

As you can see these questions are just door openers, simple enough for a young person to get started. Usually one element will become far more interesting than another but there is a broad base to begin the exploration.

For example Michael became more interested in the Mayan belief of sacrifices to appease gods, and very interested in the written language, even going so far as to find a book and to practice copying the letters and symbols.

Music

In addition to studying the arts of cultures it is important to give the opportunity for personal practice of music and art. Since we were still living in the Bay Area we continued to go to the San Francisco Symphony (SFS) performances. My friend Geraldine Walther, the principle violist in the symphony, was also in a quartet so we went to their performances as well and got to know the other musicians.

Since it was as difficult to find authentic Suzuki teachers, as it is to find authentic Montessori teachers I decided to teach Michael piano myself. I had begun piano lessons at age five with my mother and grandmother, who taught me in the traditional way. But I wanted to learn how to teach the Suzuki way. I found a book called *Studying Suzuki Piano: More than Music, a Handbook for Teachers, Parents, and Students*.

This was perfect. It was very much like Montessori. The method does not believe so much in talent as in talent education. And the activities are broken down into tiny steps that a music student can master and then build more complex skills. In the spring the international Suzuki Conference was being held in San Francisco and Jim, Michael, and I attended. Dr. Suzuki demonstrated violin lessons and I was able to attend classes given to students at all levels by Katoaka-san who was in charge of the piano part. It was quite inspiring so we started *Suzuki Book One* piano lessons right away.

Art

Until we moved to Arcata near the end of summer Michael continued art classes at Studio One in Oakland with his friends. They had experiences in weaving, collage, drawing, and painting following the method of Mona Brooks who wrote the book *Drawing with Children*.

At home it was animals, more than anything else that inspired Michael to create art.

Michael Olaf Company Selections

Here are some of the items that were added to the Michael Olaf Company catalog for this year in learning about humans: black history, US history, great women playing cards; books on prehistory, early humans, early civilizations, world history, American history, biographies; puzzle maps; books on flags, continents, the geography of the world and a children's world atlas

LANGUAGE

Reading and Literature

We continued to read together as a family in the evenings before bed, sometimes easier books, fiction and non-fiction books that we would begin and he would continue on his own the next day. The books that were added to the Michael Olaf catalog during this year provided reading exposure to many interesting non-fiction topics. Michael had discovered the *Tintin* books and graphic great literature comics and, like many children, he had first figured out the stories through the pictures, gradually reading more and more of the words.

One of his favorite comic book series was based on the Indian epic poem, *The Mahabharata*. There were 42 books in this series and they were shipped to California from India. Every few weeks when he had read the last one and saved his money we would go to the Indian store on University Avenue in Berkeley and buy the next one. The people at the store got to know Michael very well and were glad to see him coming. He went from there to reading other Indian series such as the *Ramayana*, and then European myths like *Beowulf*.

These books have stood the test of time and meet the needs to explore right and wrong, structure of communities, power, justice, and many elements of culture that are of interest to children at this age.

Writing Preparation

Aware that the development of the body, hand, and fingers is essential in creating good handwriting we were sure to include Michael in the daily practical work of the family. Artwork, weaving on a belt loom that was part of the study of cultures, building with blocks and Lego, occupied him for hours, and contributed to attractive penmanship.

Printed sheets of paper full of letters that a child has to copy repeatedly gets boring very quickly so a child will rush through these, practicing BAD handwriting, which defeats the purpose.

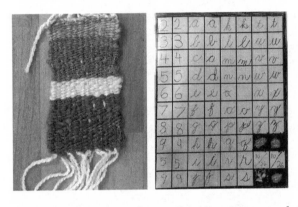

We would sometimes work together, I writing one letter slowly and carefully, followed by a discussion of what was good or not so good about how I had done the writing. When I was making a cursive "o" for example, I started the initial upstroke too high, so I crossed it out and wrote it again. This would show that even a teacher makes mistakes when not concentrating. Then Michael would carefully copy what I had written. When he was finished he often decorated the rest of the page because this was work to be proud of. In this case he decorated his work with Halloween pumpkins because it was that time of the year.

In the elementary years there is an interest in the reasons that letters are formed and then change over time, inspiring an interest in the first writing, the history of writing, where each letter came from, how language changed as humans migrated from place to place. These questions definitely add to an interest in forming letters.

Spelling Dictionary

For creative writing to be enjoyable, at any age, it is most important to get the words out of the head and down on paper, and to worry about spelling and precision later. Otherwise the thought gets blocked, interrupted by focusing on details.

As Michael began more and more to express himself with the written word we would sometimes go through a piece of his writing together and I would point out the words that were not spelled correctly. In order not to mark up a writing attempt, that took so much time and effort to create, the misspelled words were softly underlined with a pencil, not marked with red pen. Then we looked these words up in a dictionary, together at first and then Michael on his own. It helped that I am a very bad speller myself. Then I would write them beautifully in his personal *spelling dictionary* until he wanted to write them beautifully himself.

When I was teaching elementary classes my students each had their own spelling dictionary. Sometimes we could find tabbed phone number books at that time so there was a tab for each letter of the alphabet. Alternatively, as Michael and I later did, we made them, using a lined composition book and carefully measuring and cutting to create a tab for each letter.

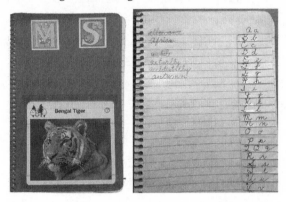

In the picture above you can see the cover that Michael created, and the tabbed page for "A a" and the words *allowance, Africa, awhile, actually, accidently,* and *autumn.* These are words that he misspelled in his own writing. He would practice writing these words until he had them memorized and then cross out the ones he knew. On this page he had memorized and crossed out *allowance, Africa,* and *awhile.*

Grammar

Michael continued the grammar exploration begun in his Kindergarten year, now using more interesting sentences from his expanding exposure to reading.

Teaching Print Letters

One day, after Michael was grown up, I asked an author to sign a book she had written, to give to another friend. She asked me, "Shall I sign it in cursive or print?" I replied, "Why do you ask?" She then enlightened me to the fact that these days when all writing is done on a computer, very few young people or adults can read cursive because they have never been exposed to it.

That year I saw some of the notes Michael had taken, in print, during law school and asked why they were so difficult to read when his cursive writing had become so beautiful. He replied, "No one can read cursive, and I never learned to print legibly."

If I had thought about this cultural change at the time, even though cursive is thought to create valuable connections in the brain, I would have taught Michael how to print as well as to write beautifully in cursive. I hope Montessori primary teachers will do this.

Michael Olaf Company Selections

Here are some of the items that were added to the Michael Olaf Company catalog for this year having to do with learning language: great authors card game; French and Spanish song and common sentence tapes; Bob Books early readers; *The Macmillan Dictionary for Children*; *Elements of Grammar*; a calligraphy kit; Brian Wildsmith early readers; Books of the Ladybird *Key Words* reading scheme from England; Ladybird abridged classics; *The Chronicles of Narnia, Beowulf, D'Aulaires' Book of Greek Myths, The legend of Odysseus*.

Artist postcard books, *Mommy, it's a Renoir* art card books; Stockmar art supplies and Prismacolor pencils; sketch books; artist/writers clip board; *The Story of Painting*

A child's xylophone, a recording of *Peter and the Wolf* and *The Young Person's Guide to the Orchestra*; tapes with the story and music of individual composers, and books about artists and musicians

MATH AND GEOMETRY

Elementary Class Math and Geometry

The 6-12 child is full of questions and wants to know the reason for everything. If we cannot explain why something is important to learn we should not be teaching it. "It will be useful some day," isn't enough.

In the Montessori elementary class the great story that introduces math and geometry takes the students back through time. Through the use of imagination, scenarios are created where counting and recording and measuring became necessary. Why is our system based on the number 10? Because we can count on 10 fingers? Why did the Egyptians use geometry? Was it to remake the property boundaries of the flooding of the Nile River? Why was it helpful to know when there would be a full moon or eclipse of the sun or moon? Having a concept of thousands, millions, billions, gives perspective in studying the timelines of the creation of the universe, the solar system, and the evolution of plants and animals. This approach opens the door to child-centered exploration of math and geometry.

We continued to make math a part of our daily lives, cooking, planning on the calendar, and math and fractions as Michael started keeping track of his allowance and expenditures.

We never required math tests or quick calculation, but suggested that every week he work through some of the Mortenson math booklets. Sadly this work seemed to fall into the same category as rote memorization, tests, and the filling in of endless math pages used traditionally, and was the least successful of Michael's homeschooling experience.

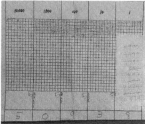

During the last semester of the first grade year, when Michael attended a Montessori elementary class, he enjoyed the Montessori materials that gave an idea of the concepts of square and cube roots, and working with counting frames. In the picture above you see him with his teacher and friends, and the "dot game" where one practices math in the decimals by filling in dots.

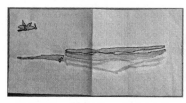

Anything connected with animals in the way of math naturally interested Michael. In the picture above he drew a picture that represents the relative sizes of a giant squid with its tentacles completely stretched out and an average size fish at the Aquarium in Golden Gate Park in San Francisco.

Next to this is a Green Peace Game he adapted to bring awareness to caring for whales. The game was full of logic, numbers, rules, and consequences of actions. Our whole family enjoyed chess and board games were an important part of our lives.

Music was also an important part of our lives. It was becoming clear that music, as well as playing games, was stimulating and improving the math brain as Michael was challenged to attend to time signatures, rhythm, pitch, intervals, formulaic progressions. When performing, he was required to concentrate on all of this at the correct speed required, especially when performing in a group. It has been shown that performing music reinforces parts of the brain used when doing math.

Michael Olaf Company Selections

Here are some of the items that we reviewed and that were included in the Michael Olaf Company catalog for this year in learning about math and geometry: Counting books from different countries in different languages; a brass traditional perpetual calendar; a book of practical story problems in number patterns, sets, probability, mileage, logic, geometry, measurement; *Family Math*, a practical math book for the home; number stamps with ink pads; a book of 3-D geometric figures to cut out and assemble; a math dictionary; these three elementary class favorites: *Number Art, Calendar Art*, and *Symbol Art*

RECORD KEEPING

Although I made suggestions, and tried to keep a balance in what Michael was offered to study, read, or research, and we had kept samples and pictures of his work throughout the year, we had no other official record-keeping system yet.

There was one exception and that was the care of animals. This was a serious responsibility. Michael made his own list of his responsibilities each day and he had a chart where he checked them off morning and evening.

Here is his list:

Mornings: feed fish, turn on aquarium light, check hermit crabs water, check bird feeder, remove cover of guinea pig cage, feed guinea pig, feed cat

Night: feed fish, turn off aquarium light, spray hermit crabs, cover guinea pig cage, put cat outside

We thought this was an excellent beginning for Michael to learn to keep records of his work, be responsible, and manage his time as we now planned to continue to homeschool, especially since it was his idea.

SECOND GRADE

Moving from the San Francisco Bay Area was definitely a transition. We found silence, solitude, nature, wild animals, the beauty of the forests and oceans, and so much more. But there was a sad part too. In this new place we had no close friends, no familiar parks and museums, no symphony orchestra. We found a much narrower cultural diversity, no Ethiopian restaurants (one of our favorite cuisines), or annual Swedish Christmas.

Michael's sisters were no longer near us. Ursula was studying in Southern California and Narda was taking her second AMI Montessori teacher-training course, for age 6-12, in Milwaukee, Wisconsin. We missed them terribly. Amidst the excitement there was pain.

Developmental Crises

I consider this experience — leaving the familiar — a *developmental crisis* for our family even though, in Montessori theory, the term *developmental crises* usually refers to the infant experiences (such as birth, weaning, and self-actualization). I remembered the words of Dr. Silvana Montanaro, head of the AMI 0-3, Assistant to Infancy training, in her book *Understanding the Human Being* about developmental crises:

> *The word "crisis" may be ambiguous, since in everyday speech it is generally used for problems. "Having a crisis" has the negative connotation of passing through a period that is full of difficulties that one doesn't know how to resolve and that are a severe trial for the*

person facing them. But this is not the original meaning of this Greek word, which means "judgment", so that "being in a crisis" implies being in a situation in which one is submitted to a test. In developmental crises, what is tested is the degree of preparation needed to progress along the path of humanization. It is rather like taking an exam. Although it is a special moment, it does not cause too many problems if you are well prepared and if the surrounding environment is supportive.

In the long process of development, a human being goes through many times of "crisis", many moments of transition between one stage of development and another. These passages are obligatory, and we cannot side step them. If everything went according to plan during the preceding phase, the person will pass the "test" without difficulty and without trauma and subsequently find himself at a more advanced phase of personal development. Not only does time pass, the chief advance is that the range of possibilities increases and the human being becomes constantly wealthier and able to participate more fully in life.

So I began to look at this period of time as painful in some ways, but as one that would open us all up to a wider possibility of exploring and enjoying life.

Human Tendencies

A very important checklist in the Montessori world is called the *human tendencies*. They exist in each individual and help one to adapt to a particular time and place. When we are creating a healthy environment for a person at any age we keep these in mind. So I thought back on this list as we continued to homeschool in this new environment. Here are some of the ones we considered:

Exploration – to research, read, learn, satisfy curiosity, explore more, in order to make logical sense.

Activity/Movement/work – to have freedom, physically and mentally to move purposefully. To have useful work to help find one's place in the family or group.

Orientation – to figure out how one fits into a particular time or environment, to be given information and opportunity but to have freedom to decide how to orient oneself to a new situation.

Order - to create an order, in time and place, through exploration and orientation. To decide where things go, material things and schedules, in order to be efficient and to feel safe and productive.

Concentration – vital for making progress in exploration and work, to be able to process incoming data and make sense of it, to think and to become fulfilled.

Imagination – this tendency is very important from age 6 or 7 on and, combined with respect for all of the other tendencies provides a way for an individual to understand the past, the present, the future, and to solve problems, to exercise independent thinking and put into reality what the imagination suggests.

Communication – this involved speaking first, in order to be able to be understood, to feel that what one has to say is valuable. Then to do the same with writing. Reading is a way to further explore, to orient oneself, to research and make sense of the world and to learn how to better express oneself.

Repetition – to return to a similar activity over and over, sometimes from a new perspective, in order to master it.

Abstraction – this could be thought of as the process of actually coming to understand something, *abstracting* an idea, and is different at different stages of life. For example the abstractions of the adjectives *large* and *small* are made clear after repeated building of the *pink tower* in the primary class. The concept or abstraction that all humans have the same physical needs becomes clear after exposure to how people in different climactic zones in the world build their homes, or what kind of food, transportation, and clothing are best for them.

Exactness/Perfection/Self-perfection – this cannot be forced with rewards or manipulation or it might be destroyed. It is important to keep in mind that working on something until it is perfect, in the way one is able to create it at the moment, is a natural human tendency. Each person must be in charge of the level of exactness they are capable of in any one moment. This applies to work attempted and to becoming the kind of person one wants to be.

So, how were we doing as a family in considering these human tendencies? Together we used all of these as we focused on rearranging and settling into a new place to live, both inside and outside of our home.

Jim's main work was involved with setting up and running the Michael Olaf Company. I had two main tasks. First of all I had learned PageMaker (the early version of InDesign) to create the *Erdkinder Newsletter*, exploring the needs of the adolescent, that I was working on with NAMTA (North American Montessori Teachers Association). Now I could begin to create the Michael Olaf catalogue in a new way, on a computer.

Of course I was very involved with helping Michael, now almost eight years old, fulfill his own needs and tendencies through exploring this new place and finding work to focus on.

Social Life

Michael was immediately engrossed with the wildlife around the house we rented that was surrounded by forests of redwood trees. And as you can surmise from the earlier chapters of this book he considered animals his friends. We woke up one night to the sound of deer munching on the corn and strawberries we had planted, and raccoons and blue jays competed with the cats for food at dinnertime.

Our close friends from the San Francisco area visited us during this first year, but as it is not easy to get to this part of the world such visits were rare and special.

In the fall of this year Ursula transferred from California College of the Arts in Oakland to Humboldt State University in Arcata. This would enable her to focus on her love of the arts and of environmental studies. And Michael had one of his sisters back.

We began to look for other activities where he would meet children, not just children exactly his age, but rather older children as models, and younger children he could help. Soon after arriving we found that there were swimming lessons at the local pool so Michael made friends that way.

On Saturdays, Humboldt State University hosted The Humboldt Music Academy on campus, with private and group classes for children age 2-18, in art, music, theatre, music history. Michael took several classes and this is where he began Suzuki piano lessons with an experienced teacher.

Carlo Mazzone-Clementi of Padua, Italy founded Dell'arte International School of Physical Theatre, here in Humboldt County. In the 1970's Jim was one of the first students so we took advantage of their excellent performances and the children's class that year.

At the end of second grade, Michael's Suzuki piano teacher, Dr. Jean Bazemore, opened The Suzuki Summer Academy in her home and Michael was probably the first person to sign up. So over the years, beginning in second grade, many of his friendships began during these music and theatre experiences.

A Part-time Homeschooling School

In the middle of the year we found out about a school for homeschoolers. "Mistwood Center for Education" was founded by two mothers whose daughters had attended a

Montessori preschool and who wanted to create the same kind of child-centered learning as they grew.

Mistwood Center
For Education
Spring 1991

The requirements for entrance were only that one must be homeschooling and must be a nice person. One could attend as little as one day or up to four days a week. Michael chose to attend once a week. He was part of this school for several years and it was a very good experience, mostly games, sports, camping and other field trips, and sometimes academic classes — everything inspired or asked for by the students who were at that time preschool or elementary age children.

Academics

Most of Michael's academic work occurred in the home and for second grade and beyond we paid attention to the human tendencies listed above, for Michael and for his parents. At home and during work trips we continued to keep in mind the Montessori structure, filling in more and more of the gaps of knowledge in the areas of Earth, Plants and Animals, Humans, Language, and Math that you will find on the next pages.

THE EARTH

Studying the earth first hand now was easy. We lived on the spot on the planet where tectonic plates met. Because the Pacific Plate was spreading, the Gorda Plate was being pushed underneath the North American Plate – and all this happening right under our home!

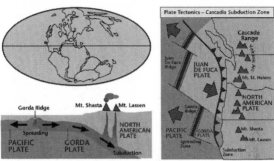

The work of wind and water, two things studied for years in the elementary class, were obvious as every time we walked on the beach the mounds of sand and the appearance or disappearance of rocks was different. It became real to think about the time in geologic history when volcanoes covered the planet because some of the rocks on the beach were obviously formed by flowing lava.

Michael Olaf Company Selections

Here are some of the items that we selected for the Michael Olaf Company catalog for this year in this area: The Earth Flag: an Ocean puzzle map; space flash cards; the electric circuit and an AC/DC card game: the Dymaxion world puzzle map (made of wooden triangles): The Peters Projection World Map large poster: Golden Guides about rocks, stars, minerals: These books: *Earth, Pangaea, 50 Simple things You Can Do to Help the Earth*

PLANTS AND ANIMALS

There was a small garden plot next to our house where we could grow vegetables but that didn't last long because the wild deer ate everything. So we planted corn and wheat in a small space, about 1.5 feet by 5 feet of soil surrounded by cement, outside the front door of the Michael Olaf store. We loved to hear parents walking past exclaim, "Is that wheat? Is that corn?" and then show the crops to their children.

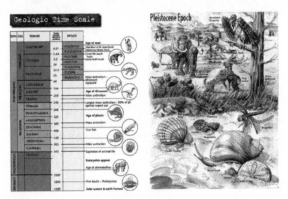

Animal Study

I kept the guidelines for the classification of animals in my mind but instead of lecturing Michael I would just mention and ask questions to myself aloud, when we encountered a new animal on land or in the tide pools at the beach:

What do they eat?

In what kind of environment do they live?

How do they reproduce?

How do they move?

How do they care for their offspring if they do?

What protects them from predators?

Animal Classification

Michael continued to collect pictures of animals of all kind to sort and add to his evolution-inspired animal classification book.

Geology and biology came together as we checked the tide tables to figure out when the minus tides would occur in order to see the most tide pool life on the beaches. The same Natural History Museum in Arcata that presented local geology provided specimens to handle, puzzles, preserved examples of local wildlife, videos, and books for the areas of botany and zoology. They gave Michael ideas of what to look for on the weekly trip to the large county library in Eureka.

As I learned to use new computer programs for our growing catalogue Michael drew the first picture for the first computer-generated cover. The drawing was made after a visit to Elk Meadow, a place not far north of us where large herds of Roosevelt Elk congregate early in the morning and at dusk.

They go where they like from Humboldt County where we live to Vancouver Island in British Colombia. There was a special radio station one could listen to when driving through the area to find out where the elk were at the moment.

Animal Dissections

Just as in my elementary classes Michael was horrified at the very idea of cutting open an animal (a fish from the market, or a bird that has flown into a window and died) to see what is inside in order to study internal organs of circulation, reproduction, respiration, and movement. But in class there are usually one or two children who get interested and then some of the others follow. Michael's sister Ursula was interested when I dissected a large bird that had flown into one of our windows. Michael peeked from a distance but couldn't bring himself to participate. We respected his choice.

He did however become fascinated in watching, for hours, a banana slug (3-6 inch creature that lives in the redwood forests) devour a mushroom. And the classification surely made him more observant of the wild and tame animals in our area.

Michael Olaf Company Selections

Here are some of the items that we approved for inclusion in the Michael Olaf Company plant and animal section of our catalog this year: leaf/flower press; children's garden book; pollination and predator card games; internal body systems cards; 3-D human body charts; dinosaur game; man of the trees video; books on fossils, tape of animal bird songs, general, and from the east and west of the USA; binoculars; animal flash card games; Books: *My Family and Other Animals* (Gerald Durrell), *The Secret Life of Plants* (recommended during my 6-12 Montessori training), *Fieldbook of Natural*

People

Field Trips

This year the Michael Olaf Company began to be invited to exhibit materials at Montessori conferences all over the country. So if there were friends we could visit where a conference was being held, Michael sometimes went along with us.

For example, both my father and his cousin were named after Clark of the Lewis and Clark expedition of 1803-1806 that attempted to find a passage through the Louisiana Purchase (a large part of the US at that time) to the Pacific Ocean. So seeing the Gateway Arch and museum where this journey began, and being able to walk the beginning of that trail, brought US History to life. We took advantage of museums in cities where conferences were being held in order to learn more about all of the academic areas Michael was exploring.

Sumeg Village

The Spanish settlers landed here over four hundred years ago but there had been Indigenous people here long before that. Just north of us there is a beautiful place called Patrick's Point State park where the Yurok tribes have built a village, Sumeg Village, exactly as they have been built for hundreds of years. Each year there is a celebration where tribal costumes made mainly of animal skin and beads and shells, and woven hats, are worn, and the traditional foods are made.

One year we went to a performance at the university of the Throat Singers of Tuva, a small country deep in the midst of Asia. They sang songs representing the sound of horses galloping across the open steppes, and at the end of the performance one man danced alone on the stage in a costume very much like those of one of the other Indigenous groups in the US. We were stunned.

This opened the door to learn about the geologic age when the Bering strait was a land bridge and people migrated from Asia over this piece of land, and then moved all over North America and on to populate South America.

The library had a very good non-fiction film collection and we brought home videos on the series *America, Civilization, King tut,* and *I Claudius.* The last, about the Roman Emperors, was very interesting but there were parts that we had to fast-forward because of the violence, so probably I wouldn't recommend it at this age unless, like Michael, a child is really interested in the Roman civilization.

Music and Art

As I said, I had taught Michael how to play the music in *Suzuki Piano Book I*, but now he had a certified Suzuki teacher. It is Suzuki practice for parents to participate in their children's lessons, so I went along, took detailed notes, and helped Michael come up with a practice plan that included time each day to listen to the tapes of professional performance of the simple piano pieces he was learning.

One day Ursula got us tickets through the university to see the pianist Peter Serkin. Michael came home after the concert and started practicing piano at 10:30 at night!

Then he became interested in and began violin lessons, and I began my own violin lessons with him. Soon Jim, who had played the violin for years but not the piano, started his own Suzuki piano lessons from Michael's teacher. Here is a note from a journal I wrote in for a short time:

> *Michael is playing lots of piano, changing everything, playing the right hand part with the left hand and the left hand part with the right hand. He tries playing with his eyes closed, and lying down (after lining up the piano bench with the sofa) so he can reach up over his head and play the piece "backwards". He doesn't know yet about major and minor keys but I hear him experimenting with changing the Suzuki pieces into minor keys.*

We found many good videos in the library and I think the movie *Amadeus*, about Mozart, inspired some of these experiments. We watched a video of Isaac Stern, the first Western musician to visit China after the Cultural Revolution and a film of Pablo Picasso actually drawing and painting!"

I thought a lot about the fact that Michael so often works like this, a way we call "thinking outside the box." Maybe it's because no one has told him, in his education so far, that there is only one way to do anything. He has been asked questions and offered ways to experiment and explore, but there have been no right way, no tests. I think this might be a result of Montessori education when it is done well.

Art was part of each day as Michael was still more interested in drawing than writing his ideas. Here is an interesting event. Michael was taking an art class but drawing really lousy stuff even though it was clear that he enjoyed spending time and doing a good job with art. So I tried tactfully to ask him why he was drawing like this. His reply? "The teacher asks the kids questions about their art and they have to answer in front of the everyone. So I just scribble." As an artist I agree with his complaint. An artist must be able to express through art, a musician through music, a writer/speaker through words.

Michael Olaf Company Selections

Here are some of the items that were tested by us and chosen to be included in the Michael Olaf Company catalog for this year in learning about humans: A world flag set of members of the United Nations; flag stickers; early picture books with simple text about the middle ages, and the civilizations of Greece, Rome and Prehistory to Egypt; biographies of great men and women; historical photograph sets; composer postcards and composer stamps; art and music card games; the following games: Ur, Senet, Go, Mankala; an aboriginal decorated Australian boomerang; an art lotto game; cassette of Teaching Peace songs; reproductions of US history documents; Where in the World geography game; Books: *Holidays around the World, The History of Everyday Things, Money, Early Humans, The Story of Painting, The Story of Music, Little House on the Prairie* books

LANGUAGE

Literature - Family Readings

Family reading together before bed was a way for Jim and me to revisit our favorite classics and to learn more through non-fiction reading. And Michael read many books that he probably would not have done if we had not begun them together. We all occasionally experimented with expression, trying to put ourselves into the voice of the person speaking so it would be interesting to listen to.

We also discovered recorded classic books. One of these was the book *Wind in the Willows*. One evening I heard the sound of this story tape coming from the bathroom. I heard the voices of Mr. Toad, Mole, and Ratty having an argument about taking a boat onto the river. I smiled remembering the scene, and then realized that Michael was in the bathtub and having a tape player plugged in near water could be dangerous. I knocked on the door and told Michael not to touch the tape recorder. There was a long silence, no sound of Mr. Toad and his friends, and then laughter. There was no tape player in the bathroom – that was Michael doing all the voices.

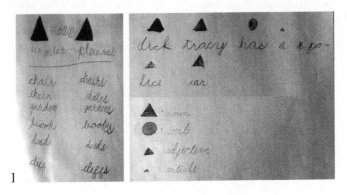

Grammar

Michael continued to study parts of speech and sentence analysis. He found it interesting that some poets use many verbs (red circles drawn and colored over the verbs made this clear) and others use more nouns (large black triangles); some poets used few, and others many adjectives (smaller blue triangles). Some writers often used the conjunction (long thin green rectangles representing conjunctions) "and", stringing sentences together making longer sentences, and some almost never used conjunctions. This made Michael aware of his own writing and use of parts of speech.

Writing

Because I was at that time creating the catalog on a computer I could experiment with different fonts. So I made stationary for all of us for writing letters. At the end of the year I left to take the first summer of the AMI Assistants to Infancy, for age 0-3, teacher-training course in Denver, Colorado. Michael wrote to me once a week over the summer on his stationary.

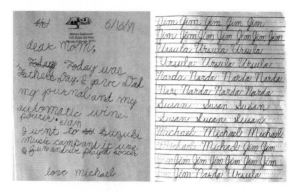

You can see in the picture that his spontaneous cursive writing was improving, and he had no problem crossing out errors rather than feeling badly about them.

His cursive writing was getting much better as long as he practiced words that were interesting, for example the names of the people in our family and the words he had recorded in his spelling dictionary and he was writing over and over to memorize.

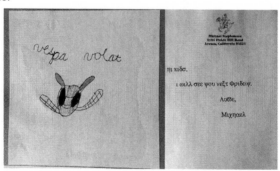

Latin and Greek

Margaret Stephenson, my elementary Montessori trainer convinced us of the importance of sharing the etymology of a word with our students, linking words we use today with how they came into use from necessity and how they were changed as languages were affected by the migrations of human groups. Both Jim and I had studied Latin in high school and I tutored high school students in the language during my freshman year of university. So we went to the library of the local high school, and then university, to find books on teaching Latin. There were none and I was shocked. This language is so interesting logically and analytically, so mathematical and satisfying. So we just focused on Latin when it came up in researching words, and Michael recorded some of his discoveries with pictures. Vespa volat in the picture above means, "The insect (It is something like a wasp) flies."

When I told him that some of my elementary Montessori students used Greek letters for writing secret code notes to each other, he found that he could change our letters into Greek on the computer. He sometimes wrote to me in Denver this way and I had to break the code.

Computer

Michael had a typing tutor game to use on our computer. There was no such thing as Internet or email then so children were not yet at risk of the addiction causing mental, social, and physical problems (of computer overuse). He only used the computer for typing tutor and sometimes writing a letter.

Expression

When I taught Montessori elementary classes we thought a lot about not only the meaning but also the emotion of words. There was a book recommended by my 6-12 trainer which I used as an example. *The Snow Goose: A Story of Dunkirk* by Paul Gallico is a heart warming story that brings tears to my eyes just remembering how my students also loved it. When these students wrote something to share with the class you can be sure they practiced their delivery, and their expression drew their audience in.

Jean Bazemore, the head of the Suzuki Summer Academy was a professor of theatre and she brought out the best of expression as the children delivered their speeches in dramas. Authentic Suzuki music also focuses on the value of playing a very few notes beautifully rather than playing many notes badly over and over in the hopes that someday it will get better. My grandmother was a musician, and seeing such emphasis on quality in both speaking and playing music reminds me of one of her favorite sayings, "Anything worth doing is worth doing well."

Michael Olaf Company Selections

Here are some of the items that were included in the Michael Olaf Company catalog for this year having to do with learning language: first grammar books such as *A Cache of Jewels* about nouns, each one filled with beautiful art and examples of the specific parts of speech, nouns, adjectives, verbs; a calligraphy kit; books: *Elements of Grammar, The Clear and Simple Thesaurus Dictionary, English Verb Conjugations, Greek Myths, The Picture Bible, The Legend of Odysseus,*

Canterbury Tales, Tales of Shakespeare, The Chronicles of Narnia, Illuminations (about the evolution and development of different fonts including the Book of Kells), *Joyful Noise* (duets of spoken expressive language)

MATH AND GEOMETRY

Practical Math

This year Michael created his first budget. He had several envelopes labeled *food, clothing, tithe, gifts,* and *toys.* On Jim's birthday he took $2.00 from his "food" envelope to help buy the food for Jim's birthday dinner. He didn't have enough money in toys to buy the pirate Lego set he really wanted so Jim paid him to put labels on the catalogs that were being mailed. He was starting to learn the value of money, especially money earned.

We didn't have Montessori math materials, but Michael had handled them in his primary years and during the semester in the elementary class, so whenever he was working on a problem that could be expressed with drawing he would record this concept or math problem by drawing in the math/geometry journal he had begun.

Michael Olaf Company Selections

Here are some of the items that we reviewed and that were included in the Michael Olaf Company catalog for this year in learning about math and geometry: a multiplication tape (valuable for children who learn better by singing than writing); Easy-to-Make 3D shapes, Count your Way around the world books – number systems from Africa, China, Mexico, Russia, others; books: *How Much is a Million, One Two Buckle My Shoe* (age appropriate exploration in counting, matching, measurement, sequencing, classification and sets, ordinal numbers, estimation, and more – practical math in the home)

RECORD KEEPING

Weekly Check-off Lists

Suzuki music lessons provided a daily check-off list that was kept on the piano, including listening to recordings. I made this list from the lesson notes and Michael checked them off. These items were always completed in order to prepare for the next lesson.

Once a week, usually on Friday at the end of the day, Michael and I jointly created a list of work for him to do or explore the following week. During the week he could add work that he did that was not on the original list; work that he didn't get to was added to the next week's list. Here is an example of one week's list:

Language: contractions, suffixes, homonyms, letter writing form, free writing with margins and indentation, spelling dictionary, dictionary

Math: multiplication, division, telling time, measuring yards and gallons, thermometer, budget, earnings

Geometry: diameter, drawing and labeling plane figures

Experiments: botany, physics

Make solar system

Prehistory

Needs of humans

Work Journals

Just as in my elementary classes Michael was the one to choose what to record in his journals, one for math (squared paper) and one for everything else (plain paper, no lines). Sometimes he would just add something to his journal every week or two, but he often would make the drawing or writing on plain paper first and then add it carefully to the journal page, often decorating the margins of the page.

We still have the Montessori elementary journals that were created by his sister Ursula during her time and they are beautiful. As I was showing them to her daughter Alexandra last year she spent a long time looking through the pages then came to Jim and me and said, "What does 'priceless' mean?"

We explained that a priceless item was something that was so special that no amount of money could match its worth.

With a soft voice full of awe she said, "These books are priceless."

THIRD GRADE

That summer we found a house for rent that was near the village of Trinidad, California. We now had neighbors. One family were homeschooling and had a boy Michael's age who was also studying Suzuki music so they became good friends. We were much closer to a community and to the beaches.

Michael's older sister Narda left at the beginning of the school year for Peace Corps training in Senegal, West Africa and then two and a half years of work as a medical volunteer in the Ivory Coast. His sister Ursula was attending Humboldt State University and volunteering to lead rafting and climbing trips for youth at risk ages 9-18. As a graduate of Montessori education from age two to twelve she was excited about the way Michael was learning and she was always glad to join in his projects and experiences.

Michael attended the Suzuki summer academy (music, theatre, Russian language, creative writing, drama, nature studies) near our home for several weeks in the summer, and a nearby theatre camp of Del Arte International. When the academic year began he returned to Mistwood (the homeschoolers group) one day a week, helped at our business, took classes from a local artist, spent Saturdays at the University Music Academy, went swimming and surfing, played soccer, and sometimes played music with friends.

 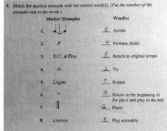

The First Test

Many of Michael's friends attended public school and he often heard them worrying about an upcoming test, something outside of his educational experience until, in a class on music theory at the Saturday Music Academy, he was given a test.

That evening as we were having dinner he said:

> *I don't see what the big deal is about tests. My friends who go to school are always worrying about them. The music test today was no problem. If I didn't know the answer to a question I just looked at the test of the person sitting next to me.*

We had to laugh and were able to explain the concept of "cheating." Michael was used to working with, not competing against, others to solve problems. This was his first experience of being asked to give information completely on his own, where his answers would be marked right or wrong by someone else, and then he might be given a grade compared to the grades earned by the other students in the class.

We explained that a test could be seen as a way to find out if a teacher was successfully imparting knowledge, and to assess the progress of a student and then give direction where he should focus his energy and time in order to improve. We explained the traditional testing situation in a positive way, but it gave us a lot to think about.

Traditional Curriculum

This led to a question of what he was studying compared to what his friends in public school were studying. I told him about my experience as a teacher in a Montessori 6-12 class. When I was teaching in California I researched the required mastery for each year from kindergarten through sixth grade. I reduced the list for each year to the minimum of one single page per grade and had the pages available at all times for the students to refer to as they made their individual weekly work plan. Just as Michael was doing, the students practiced many different schedules of how to meet these basic requirements (average two hours a week I estimated) so they would have a lot of time to follow their curiosity, just as Michael was doing.

We found the information for basic requirements for grades k-6 in California at the university. This information is easily found on the Internet today.

But actually we didn't pay much attention to these requirements because Michael was thriving and happy with the way we were homeschooling and he was learning all the time not just during what would have been "school" hours.

As Ted Dintersmith, PhD, says in his book *What School Could Be* (Princeton University Press, 2018):

> *Bulk tests don't lend themselves to higher-order competencies like creativity, communication, critical analysis, collaboration, leadership, tenacity, and entrepreneurship.*

Across America our kids study what's easy to test, not what's important to learn. It's easy to test factual content and low-level procedures, so that defines the curriculum.

We were learning that if we fed Michael's curiosity and respected his choices he enjoyed the practical work, the social interactions, the academic work, and the physical and music skills he was working on, and we believed that he had a good chance of getting good at, remembering, and being able to make use of, what he was learning. And most importantly, he would be a happy person and a contributing member of the family and his various other social groups.

THE EARTH

We continued the physics experiments on color, sound, weight, water, heat, and so on (from the book *The Red Corolla, Montessori Cosmic Education*). At a younger age these had been sensorial experiences but more and more the simple concepts opened the door to Michael wanting to know more. These experiments, and our trips to the beach, now inspired very interesting conversations and many questions: "How does the distance of the moon from earth to cause the differences in high and low tides?" "Why, as we walk on the beach, is the sound of waves louder or softer depending on where we are standing on the mounds of sand?" "Why does the heavy fog bank sit far away on the horizon until the land heats up a few miles from the coast and then come rushing in?", "What makes the colors of the sunset more vibrant after the sunsets than before?"

These were not textbook lessons but real life experiences that provided wonderful lessons of physics.

PLANTS AND ANIMALS

Because we had moved closer to the town of Trinidad it was easy to go the University Marine Laboratory that is located there. There is a picture exhibit of the years when Trinidad was a whaling town and exhibit tanks full of the kinds of sea life that exist off of its coast in the Pacific Ocean, including at times a giant Pacific octopus that was fascinating to watch whenever it came out of hiding. In the back of the building there was a tide pool touch tank where we always took visitors. Many times there were groups of children from schools who had come to see the touch tank so Michael and I gave lessons on how to pick up the creatures and very carefully and slowly return them to the tank.

This experience created more interest in animals and expanded his collection of pictures to classify into his animal classification book to include invertebrates.

 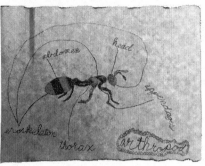

For biology assignments he wrote reports and made drawings of these and also vertebrates. If you look carefully at the picture above you can see that the edges of the paper look as though they have been burned. This was something we did in Montessori elementary classes to make a piece of work seem as though it had been created centuries ago and dug up by an archeologist. The students carefully drew and wrote on the yellowed paper (aged with a dip in tea), then rolled it up and burned the edge, creating an "ancient scroll."

People

Rome

Exploring a culture as a family can be done anywhere especially in the United States, which is a melting pot of cultures from all over the world. But one of the best things about our homeschooling schedule was that sometimes we could travel with no need to think about missing school because schooling was going on all the time, seven days a week, wherever we found ourselves.

I had completed most of the Montessori 0-3 course in Denver, Colorado and was in Rome hoping to observe the birth of a baby whose parents had been trained in the birth-preparation relaxation technique we had studied. Dr. Silvana Montanaro, the co-trainer of the Montessori course, arranged for me to observe in the hospital where she worked.

Amazingly, I was able to observe two births in the first day in the hospital so Jim and Michael and I had almost two weeks left to explore Rome.

Silvana was a passionate, enthusiastic teacher of both children and adults so we learned a lot from her, all about her family life and a lot about Italy. Michael had always lived in small one-story houses with a garden so it was fascinating to hear about how Silvana's children had grown up in an apartment, gardening in pots on the balconies, entering their home in an elevator, the elders living in the next apartment, clothing not taken to the Laundromat but washed in the kitchen and hung on the balcony to dry.

We continually referred to the civilization charts as we questioned her about how Romans meet their needs of food, shelter, transportation, and clothing, and the mental and spiritual elements of life.

We were staying not far away in a tiny room in a convent with three tiny beds so close together that we had to climb into them from the ends, and a shower so small that if anyone dropped the soap they had to get out of the shower in order to be able to bend over to pick it up. Breakfast was coffee, hot milk for Michael, and bread and butter and we went to the outside market for fruit and cheese and more bread freshly baked for lunch.

Michael had brought his violin and there was a piano so he was invited to play for the children who attended the preschool at the convent. He really enjoyed the fact that when he played music by the composers in the Suzuki repertoire, all of whom were European, the children knew the melodies and hummed along with big smiles on their faces.

Silvana became so involved with our culture research that she took us to her favorite churches in Rome, explained what else we should see and how to get to these places by bus, and invited us for pizza with another Montessorian Gianna Gobbi. One day she drove us to Ostia Antica, an archaeological site near the port of Rome and loved explaining to Michael the details of life at that time, from how food was prepared to how the toilets worked.

Sofia Cavalletti and Gianna Gobbi had years earlier created a program for teaching religion to children in the Montessori way, with sensorial materials for the youngest, timelines and other materials for the older children. This program, called The Catechesis of the Good Shepherd, is now taught all over the world and I have seen beautiful catechesis environments for children of all ages in the United States, Colombia and Ecuador.

Silvana met weekly with adolescents to discuss Catholicism at their stage of life and she took us with her during our visit. Since Michael was already so interested in the Bible the timing was perfect and the teacher loved talking to him. She gave him an elementary class project: looking at the picture in a book for guidance, he placed labels on a printed map of the parts of the city of Jerusalem, and then was instructed to copy the labels to create his own map. When the teacher asked Sofia what to do because the labels were all in Italian Sofia said, "He can write them in Italian." This was a precious keepsake of our trip.

When we returned home after this trip Michael read his first non-fiction historical novel, *I, Claudius*, reading every day until he finished this book over 450 pages in length! *I, Claudius*, written by Robert Graves, is in the form of an autobiography of the Roman Emperor Claudius and is a great introduction to Roman history.

Michael and Babies

During the academic year, as part of the Montessori 0-3 course I was taking, I observed 350 hours of babies and children of several different ages and stages of development in various environments. Michael went with me. I was focused on making detailed notes on the babies, the environments, and the parents. Michael was usually concentrating on work he had brought along. But if there was a piano he would play and we would watch to see how the infants reacted. They always paid attention and one little girl loved to climb up on the piano bench and help Michael play.

a farewell, until later, concert for
Kino
from his friend
Michael
October 11, 1994
Trinidad, California

Gigue from Partita in B flat
&
Gavotte
J.S. Bach

One little boy became quite attached to Michael. They became friends and Kino and his mother sometimes visited us. A few years later, when Michael found out that the family were going to move out of the area, he designed and printed a lovely music program, invited the family to our home, and gave Kino a private good-by concert that was very touching for all of us.

LANGUAGE

Literature - Family Readings

Here is a list of some favorite books Michael recorded in his journal this year: *The Mahabharata* (comics from India), *Sherlock Holmes Case Book, Beowulf* and *The Legend of Odysseus* (children's versions), *Dances with Wolves, The Picture Bible, Story of the Theatre, The Sailor Who Captured the Sea, Tales of Long Ago, One Day in Ancient Rome, The Story of Numbers, Lafcadio* (Shel Silverstein), *The Brothers Lionheart, The Llama and the Great Flood, This is Paris, Wild Places,* all *Tintin* Books (we discussed the prejudices and stereotypes that are often found in *Tintin* books when they came up), Ladybird abridged classics from England: *The Tale of Two Cities, The Tinderbox, Tom Sawyer,* and *The Christmas Carol*

Report Writing and Grammar

All through Michael's years of homeschooling we looked for inspiring figures in all areas throughout history to serve as models of being good and helpful people. Gandhi, Mother Teresa, Jesus, Martin Luther King, Jr, and others. To remember these figures sometimes Michael wrote about them.

In this picture you can see that he used selections from his readings to explore grammatically, in this case adding the parts of speech symbols to God's words to Abraham from the Bible. During this year Michael became very interested in the picture Bible his grandmother had given him and carried it around with many post-its sticking out of the pages marking things he wanted to discuss.

Michael sometimes compared it to what he was reading in the Mahabharata comics and learning in evolution studies. These were very interesting conversations that encouraged more research.

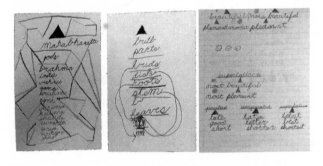

The noun study reflected what he was interested in, for example above the characters in the Indian epic *The Mahabharata*, the parts of a flower bulb, and positive, comparative, and superlative versions of adjectives, These were words that he might use in his own writing.

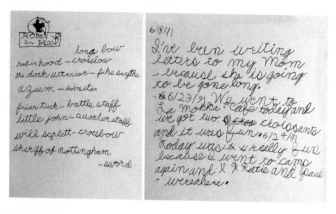

Free Writing

We did not require writing but suggested things to write about. Above is a picture he drew of Robin Hood and made a list of the weapons used by the characters in the Robin Hood book. He wrote in a journal when we went places, had company, or sometimes just a daily journal for a few days.

Beautiful Handwriting

The Montessori way is to help children to be able to write in such a way that they can be proud of their penmanship. This is done by giving many kinds of eye-hand control activities, providing age-appropriate and enjoyable ways to practice writing beautiful letters, and — rather than requiring repetitive writing worksheets — watching for when children are ready, express an interest, and can write using their own words and stories.

The picture below shows a writing example of one of our grandchildren who was visiting us years later. She was, at that time, in the same writing stage as Michael now. She asked me for some text in print that she could try to turn into cursive.

I gave her several and was delighted to see that her choice was about the Tibetan figure the Medicine Buddha.

MATH AND GEOMETRY

1- uno		9- nueve	
2- dos		10- diez	
3- tres		11- once	
4- quatro		12- doce	
5- cinco		13- trece	
6- seis		14- quatorce	
7- siete		15- quince	
8- ocho		16- diez y seis	

Math of Other Cultures

Many of the cultures Michael became interested in had different ways of expressing, and different names, for numbers. Inspired by our trip to the Yucatan peninsula and exposure to the Mayan civilization of Mexico, one of the entries in his journal recorded the Spanish words for the numbers from one to ten, and the way these numbers were represented by the ancient Mayans.

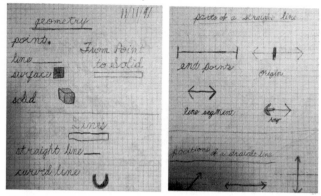

Geometry

When we unpacked boxes from my teaching years we found a set of geometry booklets that I made during my 6-12 training and the following teaching years. Michael decided he wanted to learn all of them and to help with the learning he began with the first books, drawing the illustrations and labels in his math journal.

RECORD KEEPING – TIME MANAGEMENT

Suzuki music practice required a daily music schedule check-off list. For other areas of homeschooling Michael and I discussed different ways to fulfill responsibilities, schedule work, and plan time. Jim and I had our own systems of keeping track of work and events and Michael decided to try this commercially available weekly list.

He picked one or two main work items for each day and made a little circle after each to fill in when it was completed. Sometimes it was just reading in a book (botany on Thursday); sometimes he did more and added circles (math connected with our store); and sometimes he crossed out the assignment and replaced it with what he actually did (Friday history, crossed out "dinosaur book" and added "Rome".

This is very similar to what a Montessori teacher's records look like for an individual child in a primary class, lessons suggested to be offered, and then a record of the work that was actually chosen by the child and completed.

FOURTH GRADE

This year Ursula and her many friends were in Trinidad and Michael became very comfortable with college students, playing music, games, and going to the beach. Also the daughter of my good friend, Montessori teacher Robin Renshaw, joined us once a week. Katie was two years older than Michael and had never been to a Montessori elementary class so it was very nice to see Michael share what he was learning with her and to watch them explore chess, cooking, and academics together.

Writing Resistance

Sometimes I worried that Michael was not writing as much as he would have been in a Montessori or traditional school. Then at a homeschooling talk we met Ned Colfax, son of the famous homeschooling family whose story is shared in the book *Hard Times in Paradise*. Michael told Ned that he didn't like to write as much as his parents thought he should.

After a conversation on the subject Ned wrote this in the front of the book:

> *To Michael, I did not start writing until I was 14*
> *years old because there was nothing I was interested in*
> *writing about. However, now I cannot stop writing and*
> *love to write all the time. I guess I didn't use up my*
> *writing desires when I was little. If you go to law school,*
> *look out; I had to write 7 hours of exam essays in one day.*
> *You have to love writing to enjoy that. Good Luck. Ned*

I should not have worried. Michael also went to law school and loved to write; he was an editor of the law review at his school.

 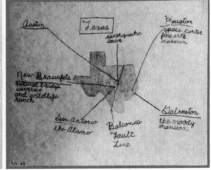

Writing about Texas

Grandparents from both sides of the family were in Texas at the same time this year so Jim and Michael and I went to visit. It was wonderful to be with family since we are spread so far and wide, but this trip was also a confirmation of what can happen when children are not forced. Michael exploded into writing! He made a descriptive map of the state showing places we had visited, and filled pages and pages of his journal, during and after this trip, with memories, stories, observations on The Natural Bridge Caverns, a wildlife ranch, Balcones fault line, The Alamo, and the Houston Space Center.

This is our room at the Montessori Training Center in Hampstead. Narda and Susan both studied here.

Scotland and England

The highlight of this year was a trip to Scotland and England. Michael was invited to be in a play in the Edinburgh Fringe Festival with the Sequoyah Theatre of California. Michael and I flew to London and took a train to Edinburgh, stopping in York to see the Jorvik Viking Center, which was important as Jim's family originally came from Norway. After the many days of rehearsal and performance in Edinburgh we took the Night Scotsman overnight train (partly for the experience of being served tea in our bunk beds in the morning) and then the underground to the Maria Montessori Institute where both Narda and I had taken our first AMI Montessori courses, Narda in 1993 and I in 1971.

Because the school term had not yet begun we were able to sleep in the office, cook our meals in the kitchen, and visit friends. From there we traveled all over London for days — another revelation — Michael had become interested in everything! I could hardly keep up with his desires to explore. We took a tour of Buckingham Place and the changing of the guards, the Tower Bridge and London Dungeon, and the Victoria and Albert and other museums. All were his choices.

Museums

When taking children to a museum I would have a plan depending on the children. For example in a primary class I would go to the museum ahead of time and find out what would be interesting for this age; then plan something specific to look for in paintings — animals, or food, or children (just one) — in order to give a focus to our trip.

Upon entering the museums with Michael we went first to the museum store, looked through the museum catalog or the exhibit postcards if they were available, and made a list of what he wanted to see. I was often surprised at his choices because, as he generally explored history and politics with Jim, he knew more about some of the exhibits than I did, and was able to teach me as much as I taught him as we roamed the halls of the museums.

I will include details further in this chapter.

THE EARTH

Returning from Texas Michael was very interested in learning more about space and the earth. One of the largest rooms of the caves at Natural Bridges Caverns is the size of a football field and one stands below giant stalactites that took millions of years to form, one drop at a time. The Balcones Fault in Texas has been dormant for 15 million years so Jim and Michael (not I!) felt safe descending into the earth in a cave caused by earthquakes, and looking up to see a crack in the earth's surface, a fault line, on the ceiling above them.

After the visit to the Space Center in Houston, Michael created a graph that showed the relative temperatures of the planets in our solar system, and drew pictures of the simple physics experiments he carried out.

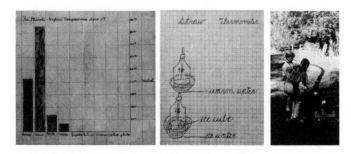

The Black Strip

The Black Strip is a piece of Montessori elementary material that Michael was happy to share with Katie. Together they created a volcano from Papier-mâché, and then stretched out the black Pellon[tm] strip that I had from my teaching days.

There is a story of how Montessori first gave this lesson. She and her son Mario were in India working on the development of the elementary curriculum and she wanted to give an idea of the history of the earth related to the existence of humans.

She had a seamstress create a long black strip of fabric, almost 1000 feet long. Then she had it wrapped around a wooden dowel and stretched between two bicycles. Two teachers slowly drove their bicycles down the street unrolling the cloth as Montessori walked along saying nothing, the children following and becoming more and more curious.

Finally at the end the children could see there was a small strip of cloth that was a different color. Montessori explained that the black represented how long the earth had existed, and the colored part represented how long there have been humans on earth.

With Michael and Katie I told the story of the first great lesson, the creation of the earth, placing the volcano—and "exploding" it—about where on the length of the strip the earth would have been covered by volcanoes for so long. After we unrolled the strip and saw the little colored strip at the end we went to the beach.

There we stood together where the ocean meets the sand, where we could see nothing of humans, no cars, no people, no structures, nothing. We imagined what the earth must have been like when there was only water and earth, where the waves over millions of years had broken the rocks into tinier and tinier pieces eventually making sand like that we were standing on.

This is one example of how the elementary child reaches out into the past and through space with the powerful imagination functioning at this age. And then wants to know more.

PLANTS AND ANIMALS

Plants

Katie's father was very knowledgeable about the local mushrooms. He took us on walks to identify and gather them and then back to the house where we learned more from his books, and cooked them for lunch.

Transferring plants from the wild to see if they could survive in the garden, what their needs were as far as sunlight and water, and then drawing and recording their growth intrigued Michael. And he continued the botany experiments (that are described in the book *The Red Corolla* book), observing over time and recording the results in his journal.

Although he was past the stage of just wanting to know the names of leaf shapes (that children learn in the primary classes) he became interested in other related characteristics. He drew pictures and labeled examples of simple or compound leaves, pinnately compound (vetch), and palmately compound (lupine). As I was taking a class on local herbs, identifying, gathering, and making teas and tinctures, Michael joined some of the classes. Then he gathered some wild plants from the woods and grew them in the garden.

Michael really enjoyed sharing his leaf/flower press, and the animal classification book he created over the years, with Katie.

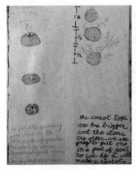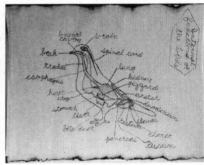

Finally he was over his abhorrence for dissection of found animals and became very interested in discovering the internal parts of a bird that had flown into a window of the house. We had long discussions about how the internal organs of a bird were related to those of humans, and how they function. The discussion naturally moved to the internal organs of the animals in his classification books—which organs evolved first and why, following the evolution of animals from the very beginning to the future. And "what will happen to bodies in the future?" was his next question.

I told him about the ideas of Dr. Montanaro, my Montessori 0-3 trainer, who says if we continue to experience reality through screens, and do all of our work on computers, humans of the future might have large mouths, very large hands, and very small and weak bodies. No one knows.

Gathering butterfly and moth cocoons, caring for them until they hatched, and releasing them inspired learning more about the kinds, and reasons, for the Latin names given to them.

Natural History Museum, London

While we were in London we spent a lot of time in the zoology area of the Natural History Museum. After having spent months collecting pictures and classifying animal according to eras on the evolution timeline, seeing the actual animals was fascinating. Michael was able to see part of a Tyrannosaurus rex, the skull of a triceratops, a blue whale model hanging from the ceiling, a giant squid, insect models as large as Michael, and actual specimens collected by Charles Darwin. Although we had looked through the postcards in the store before exploring the museum, Michael collected many more before leaving and added them to his animal classification book when we were home.

Just as in the Montessori class, I never knew where the direction of interest in biology might go next, and I enjoyed learning along with this student.

PEOPLE

Fuenteovejuna

As I mentioned in the beginning of this chapter, Michael was part of a group from the Humboldt State University's Sequoyah Theatre of California invited to perform at the Edinburg Fringe Festival this year.

The play chosen by their director, Jean Bazemore, *Fuenteovejuna* was written by the Spanish playwright Lope de Vega and first published in Spain in 1619. It is about the class struggle between a powerful commander and inhabitants of the village *Fuenteovejuna* and is based on a real event. Even women's rights are explored which is rare for something written at that time.

Our actors rehearsed for many days. As was the case for all actors, from all over the world, gathering in Edinburgh and competing for audiences, they were also required to dress up and perform skits and hand out fliers inviting the people to come and see their play. This was a valuable experience for Michael and his new friends in many ways.

"The prison, where we did our best performance"

Prison and Compassion

While in the midst of rehearsals at the Edinburgh Fringe Festival our theatre company were invited to perform at the men's prison in Cambridge, UK. We drove from Edinburgh to Cambridge, passing Hadrian's Wall on the way, for a very special weekend performance.

With the exception of two fourth graders (Michael and his friend Andrea) and one senior, the actors were students at Humboldt State University. After the performance, we all visited and spoke with the prisoners. Putting on the play and speaking with the men afterward was an emotional and educational experience for everyone involved.

These men were imprisoned for life but as they talked to the students it became clear that they were just people. The conversations were honest and important. And as we left, and the heavy doors clanged shut behind us, the students realized that many of these men would never again be able to leave this building or to have a normal life with their families. Many of the students burst into tears.

Just as our family had found as we fed the homeless at the Eureka Rescue Mission here at home, people are people. The homeless were often in this situation because of a family crisis and having no health insurance. Or because there had been a death in the family and he or she was unable to get back to a normal life.

I think such experiences make everyone involved think twice before classifying people according to their ethnicity, country, economic situation, or because they are in jail; and perhaps have a bit more compassion for others.

While in London we visited the Wax Museum. Although I knew many of the famous figures, Michael knew more, because of the interest in history and politics he shared with Jim, and he wanted to have his picture taken with some of them. The first picture above was taken at the home of Sherlock Homes. The home was so well put together, so authentically following the stories, that we could understand why there were letters on display from people around the world who thought Sherlock Holmes was a real person instead of a creation of Sir Arthur Conan Doyle. The picture of Michael with Gandhi was his favorite and our choice for this year's Christmas card.

Michael's interest in ancient civilization continued. One day he and some neighbors who were also interested in the history of Greece and Rome built a model of the city of Troy on the beach. I took pictures and asked Michael to make a map of Europe showing Troy, and we included the pictures on the cover of the Michael Olaf catalog that year.

Michael had been introduced to the flags of the world in his Montessori class. This year he decided to record color-pencil drawings of the countries he knew something about.

Art and Music

While in Edinburgh the musicians in town for the festival performed daily, even a group of Andean musicians from South America.

This year Michael continued Suzuki piano and violin and started keeping programs and brochures from special concerts and exhibits: Oakland Interfaith Gospel Choir with the Arcata Interfaith Gospel Choir performance; An Afternoon in Vienna (Humboldt State University musicians); *California Generations*

(California Native American music and dance, an historic statewide tour): *From Women's Hands*, Native American Basketry; *Hamlet* and *Les Miserables* (both seen in London); *Fuente Ovejuna* by Lope de Vegas (seen at our university before he was part of the performance in Edinburgh).

In London we spent a lot of time at the National Gallery. Michael was already interested in art and had been exposed to artists and even my own art, as I am a painter. He collected postcards of his favorites and when home pasted them into an album and labeled them. Above are a few, but others included: Poussin, Leonardo da Vinci, Rembrandt, Turner, Botticelli, Monet, Rousseau, Van Gogh, Degas, Renoir, Picasso, Seurat, and Holbein.

The third great lesson given at the Montessori elementary stage of development, when students study the needs of humans and the development of civilizations and the arts, provided enthusiasm and information to build on for some time.

LANGUAGE

For some reason Michael became very interested in this poem and the illustrations of Samuel Taylor Coleridge. So much so that he copied much of the poem in his work journal. His grammar work became more interesting as he took the sentences from his readings and made very nice drawings to illustrate.

His drawing, writing, and handwriting were improving, partly because of all of the interesting experiences he had to remember and to share this year.

The experience of being part of the play *Fuenteovejuna* in Edinburgh broadened Michael's ideas of the power of literature. He had encountered it in reading, but being part of a powerful emotional play as part of the cast, and experiencing the emotion performing it at the men's prison, made the potential of spoken and written words and sentences very clear.

One day at the end of the year, as Michael was looking through our bookcase, he discovered the book *Claudius the God*, a companion to the book *I, Claudius* that he had read last year. He was so pleased and came to us very excitedly, "Why didn't you tell me there was another book about Claudius!" and started reading it immediately. It was a closure for him, as both books are covered in the video Masterpiece Theatre miniseries *I, Claudius* which we had all watched.

We continued to have family readings in the evenings but at this point we had to wait until he was finished reading *Claudius the God.*

Math and Geometry

Michael continued keeping track of earnings, budget, and opened his first checking account, actually writing his first check to pay for the Suzuki Summer application.

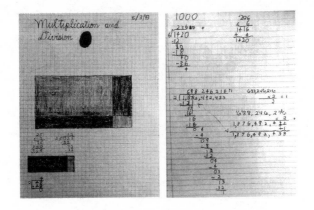

He linked practice in basic arithmetic skills to the visual, recording some of the problems that he enjoyed in his math journal. These were usually large problems that were connected to something he was interested in.

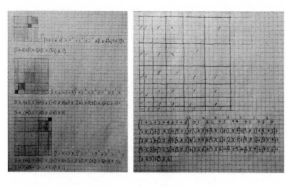

He also recorded some of the algebra problems in his math journal.

RECORD KEEPING

Journals

Over the years Michael tried many different systems of keeping track of work and meeting goals. For a while this year he sat down at the end of each day and remembered what he had worked on and made a list in a work journal. Here is a list of some of the things he would record at the end of day, one of his experiments in record keeping:

4/26/93

1. Played Nectar collector game

2. Drew a picture of a bee

3. Read Peer Gynt story

4. Made tofu burgers for lunch

5. Read Hamlet

6. Played piano duets with Katie

7. Cleaned out the wood shed

Here are some examples of activities that Michael recorded on his recordkeeping chart, usually at least four or six competed each day:

> Played chess, fixed deviled eggs and polenta for lunch, timeline of life, Pied Piper of Hamlin by Robert Browning, Ivan stories of old Russia, algebra squares, bird dissection, parts of the bird scroll, carved pumpkin and roasted seeds, kinds of water forms, ground wheat for chapattis, capitals of the world, pick herbs for tea, winter solstice, wash dishes, The Highwayman by Alfred Noyes, typing tutor, Native American groups map, fixed sushi for lunch, read evolution book, fed Chelsea's animals and collected eggs, sentence analysis, planted tropical vine seeds with Ursula

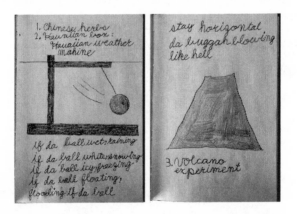

Michael's journals presented a combination of what he was doing, what he valued, and sometimes, who he was. He was often voted funniest person in various music, school, soccer, and other groups of friends. Above is a picture of two of the pages in a journal kept this year.

Practical Life – Preparation for the Present

You will notice that Michael's work included a lot of activities that in Montessori we call *practical life* work. This work is very important at all ages for several reasons:

1 – To help a person focus on the present instead of thinking that schoolwork is all for "some day in the future." This is especially important in times of political stress or worry about the environment.

2 – To help a person feel value now as a contributing member of the family, and society.

3 – To provide a balance between the mind and the body and the spirit, developing all three.

4 – To give a person the skills that help one to become a responsible and helpful friend, family member, sibling, and partner. What good is spending all of one's schooling developing the mind if one cannot be a contributing member of one's family and society.

FIFTH GRADE

In Montessori philosophy we speak often of following a child's instincts, for the child to learn to achieve balance in life. It is common to see a child sit quietly for long periods of time and then stand up, look around the room, and attempt a challenging physical activity. Or we see a child concentrate on one subject for a long time (hours in the primary class, days in the elementary class) and then move on, often with no direction from an adult, to another subject on which to concentrate. We can call this *flow*.

In the fifth grade year Michael continued to change his focus and interests. Last year, even though the travel to countries and museums was only a few weeks in total, these experiences were extremely intense and rich, and inspired much of the work this year.

There were two main interests this year. First of all Michael began to integrate, to make sense of and calmly explore, all of the information and experience from last year.

Secondly, he began to concentrate more on learning to use and strengthen his body, through swimming, riding horses, river rafting, soccer, martial arts, and music.

Hwa Rang Do

Michael participated in the Humboldt Youth Soccer League all year and Jim and I were typical parents attending games and cheering them on.

Then Michael heard about a very special Hwa Rang Do master who was teaching children. Mr. Perez, a music instructor at Eureka and Arcata high school and a first-degree black belt in Hwa Rang Do, a Korean martial art that integrates mental and physical discipline, was teaching children and adults five nights a week.

Before accepting a student Mr. Perez made sure they were interested in developing patience, respect, and self-discipline, not in learning a violent sport. The students called him "sir" and periodically he sent a questionnaire home to be sure they were doing their homework (they could do it before the class in the dojo if necessary), helping with chores, keeping a clean room, and being polite. These actions were considered a reflection of the inner discipline of Hwa Rang Do, a discipline, he teaches, that takes a lifetime to master.

In one way this was very much in line with Michael's education (valuing practical life, politeness, and being challenged to perfection and self-discipline) and in another way the opposite (being publicly corrected and calling the teacher "sir"). But we were lucky to have this teacher in the community and Michael worked hard and took this learning very seriously

Music

While visiting my family in Florida, whom Michael didn't get to see very often, he was able to experience two new instruments. My mother had played the harp since she was a child and my younger brother Tim started playing the drums when he was young and was still playing. You can read a little more about this visit in the language section of this chapter.

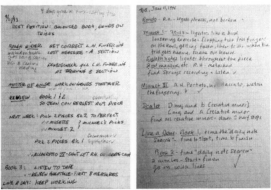

As Jim and I were studying piano (Jim) and strings (I was learning viola) along with Michael, we considered it a gift to take detailed notes at his lessons—as a parent is supposed to do in the authentic Suzuki system of learning music. You can see examples of our notes, Jim's violin lesson notes and my piano lesson notes, in the picture above.

Back at home, on Michael's first practice day, we would go over the notes together just to be sure we all understood what they meant, and then help Michael transfer the assignments to his weekly list for the following week. Eventually he was completely in charge of this last part even though we took the notes for several years.

What if a Student Wants to Quit?

All through this book you can see that we didn't reward or penalize in order to get Michael to work or study. So what did we do when he tired of practicing? We figured it out.

The deal we made was that he could stop studying any instrument; it was his choice. But to be fair to the teacher, so that he or she could fill that lesson slot with a student on a waiting list, he had to give the teacher a month's notice. He agreed. Through the years, no matter what the problem was that had made him want to quit, it resolved itself before it was necessary to give notice.

THE EARTH

Physics on the River

I continued to show Michael the physical science experiments mentioned in the last chapter and he carried out other experiments from library books.

However, the opportunity to work with his sister Ursula (who was a river guide) on river trips provided valuable first-hand experience in learning about the physical world, the wind, water, rivers, rocks and rapids, and the sky.

It requires skill to prepare the rafts in such a way as to balance the weight when tying down the equipment in case the raft capsized. In planning when to stop and set up camp—putting up tents, building fires, cooking, cleaning up, preparing for night—it was necessary to pay close attention to the weather and the time of day, attention to light, sound, water, temperature, fire, weight, movement, and more.

The river rafting experiences that began this year made Michael very appreciative of the beauty of nature and of the importance of protecting wild environments that have been almost untouched by humans. They would spend several days at a time traveling through just such places on rivers. Michael studied, eventually developed an interest in, and wrote a report on, rainforests of the world.

This is from his journal:

A few days ago Ursula and I went on a three-day rafting trip. You could almost only hear and see water. We saw a bald eagle at lunch and a deer and an otter while we were on the river. The deer was the closest.

In one of my Kids Discover *magazines there was an article about the Rain Forest. A few weeks ago I gave $14.00 to help buy the rain forest and mom gave $14.00 too.*

PLANTS AND ANIMALS

Wild Plants

I was taking a course on wild plants of the North Coast of California, and Michael often went with me to our classes and field trips. At home we made teas from herbs we gathered, which interested Michael. He collected, pressed, and researched some of the plants for his journal. I learned a lot from his research. For example "Oxalis", the scientific name for Redwood Sorrel, means *sour*. And the leaves are indeed sour. The name "Lupine" means, "wolf" and "Trillium", a spring flowering plant with three leaves and three petals, means "threes".

A Rotten Jaw Bone from Africa

One day as we stopped at the post office to get the mail we were met by the front desk clerk with a request to quickly remove a package we had received from Africa that was smelling up the small building!

It did indeed smell very bad so we put it in the trunk of the car and drove directly home. Opening it with care (outside) we found a rotting bone. We put it in the woods far from the house and opened the accompanying letter from Narda (outside).

Narda, like us, had been a vegetarian. But it was impossible for her to get many vegetables in the villages where she was working, so she had to eat meat. One day she fished an interesting-looking bone out of her stew that seemed to be the jawbone of a medium-size mammal. It was too large for a rat and too small for a dog. She thought it would make a good homeschool project for Michael to identify it. It was too late. We had to throw it out.

Dead Raja Inornata

One day we found a dead California skate on the beach. This is a type of cartilaginous fish or ray. Rather then take a picture of it to put into Michael's animal classification book we decided to take it home to possibly be dissected. It took both of us to get it into the trunk of the car. By the time we arrived home it had become clear that we had to put it somewhere away from the house for a few days or weeks till it dried out and stopped smelling. When we went back a few days later to check it had been eaten.

 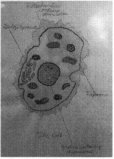

Kélé Comes from Africa

In the spring of the year, Narda and Ulysses arrived in the US from Africa. Narda had brought her dog Kélé that she had adopted to guard her house in Abidjan, Côte d'Ivoire. She asked that we bring him home with us.

Kélé became deeply ensconced as a member of our family and became one of Michael's more important and most enjoyable responsibilities. You can see a painting I did of the two of them on the cover of this book.

Also in the picture you can see a drawing of a cell. The science fiction book *A Wrinkle in Time*, by Madeleine L'Engle, tells the story of a boy whose mitochondria, the powerhouse of a human cell, is beginning to die. It is a fascinating book and inspired Michael to know more about our cells. One never knows where an interest will be born.

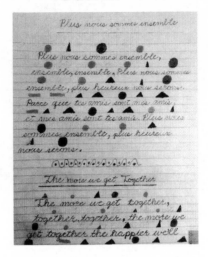

Because Narda was communicating in French in Africa Michael became interested in studying this language. We got tapes and books and videos from the public library, and since Jim and I had both studied French we tried it out a bit at home, not to master French but for fun.

The father of one of Michael's best friends, Gabriel, was from France. They traveled to France often and spoke French at home. So we made a deal. One night a week Gabriel would stay overnight with us and we would help him with his writing. And once a week Michael would stay overnight with them and they would speak only French. It was really a wonderful experience for us all. Gabriel and Michael are still very close as adults.

Young Indiana Jones

Keeping the third great lesson in mind, where one studies civilizations through explorations of the physical and spiritual needs, talking about history and culture was part of our everyday conversations. Michael was still interested in the Greeks, the Romans, and the Maya, and in the countries he had visited last year.

This interest expanded exponentially after the discovery of the *Young Indiana Jones* videos from the TV series that was filmed beginning in 1992. Sadly in 1993 it was discontinued because there was not enough interest.

I must say that I enjoyed learning about history from these videos as much as Michael. And Jim knew so much about history that he was able to fill in the details for us.

The series was filmed in various places, all over Europe and in Egypt, India, and China. Historical figures featured on the show included Leo Tolstoy, Howard Carter, Charles de Gaulle, John Ford, T. E. Lawrence, Pancho Villa, Edgar Degas, Giacomo Puccini, George Patton, Pablo Picasso, Eliot Ness, Al Capone, Annie Besant, Jiddu Krishnamurti, Norman Rockwell, Louis Armstrong, George Gershwin, Winston Churchill, Ho Chi Minh, Carl Jung, Sigmund Freud, Ernest Hemingway, Albert Schweitzer, Mata Hari, Nikos Kazantzakis, and Theodore Roosevelt.

The stories were imaginary but so much based on fact that it made one have more of an idea of the periods of history and the players.

This year Michael wrote in his journal:

> *When I grow up I want to be an archeologist, a soccer player, and a musician.*

LANGUAGE

As I have said, over the years Jim and I went back and forth in our feelings that homeschooling was wonderful and that homeschooling was not such a great idea.

For a short time this year, worried that he was again not writing enough, especially since he had begun to write so much last year, I asked Michael to put on his weekly list "Write 100 words a day." I did this because once when I was in high school and couldn't get started on a paper assigned for school my father's advice was just to start writing, writing anything, and then the thoughts would start to come. But that obviously wasn't working for Michael. I found this note in his journal,

> *I do not like to write because mom makes me write a certain number of words, which makes me mad and that's why I hate writing. Mom makes me write one hundred words. I wish I could write as much as I want. I'm still not finished because I haven't written a hundred words. (That is 54 words.)*

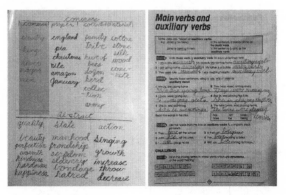

Michael always seemed to be interested in the structure of language, words that could be more than one part of speech, nouns of different kinds such as abstract and concrete. I was guiding him according to my Montessori teacher training and experience but sometimes we would go to a school supply store and buy some math or language workbooks for him to feel like he was having the same experience as his friends.

Books

Here are some favorites recorded in Michael's journal this year: *Sounder, Dragonwings, The House of Sixty Fathers, Julie of the Wolves, The Big Wave, Saturnalia, Journey to Jo'burg, Rescue, The Upstairs Room, The Black Stallion Mystery, Captains Courageous, 20,000 Leagues Under the Sea, The Brothers Lionheart Jurassic Park, A Wrinkle in Time, Wind in the Door, Claudius, the God*

Music

This summer he attended the Suzuki Summer Academy for six weeks and continued violin and piano lessons. At the Children's Music Academy on Saturdays he also took six-week classes such as street samba, Haitian dance, junior orchestra, mallet ensemble, and Orff. I had begun to teach him folk guitar, an instrument I had picked up by ear, but already he knew more than I did—for example the names of the chords! Then he signed up for a class at the Music Academy on classical guitar.

Whenever we visited Michael's grandparents he would prepare a concert ahead of time and we would make a program on the computer. These were his gifts to them.

During one visit my mother made copies of the program and gave them to friends and Michael played violin and piano for them. I am pretty sure he would have been too shy to do this had it not been for his Suzuki experience, during which a student who can only play three notes on the violin still gets to dress up, perform those three notes, take a bow, and receive applause.

After the performance he was asked to sign the guests' programs. That was a surprise and a first experience and he didn't mind because his grandparents were all, by then, very proud of his beautiful handwriting.

Music Composition

Just as I had done with students in my Montessori elementary classes I suggested that Michael, who wanted to make up his own music and write it down, begin with copying out the simple compositions of other people. Today, in 2020, Michael is still enjoying composing music.

MATH AND GEOMETRY

Michael was earning money at our company both at the store and when he helped with conference exhibits. He, with our suggestions, developed an elaborate system for keeping track of his earnings. A special notebook contained a ledger page and envelope for each category. In the spring of the year, just before we were leaving to visit my parents in Florida, he wrote in his journal how much money he had in each category in case he wanted to spend some during the trip. Here are some examples.

Toys: $36.00

Books: $4.00

Clothing: $29.00

Education: $14.00

Entertainment: $9.00

Food: $2.00

Gifts: $12.12

Tithe: $26.60

Music: $23.00

Savings: $61.00

When I shared this project with other Montessori teachers I was asked to write an article about it. It was shared at many Montessori schools. Here are some excerpts from that article:

Age Appropriate Budgeting

When Michael wanted to buy something he figured out how he could earn the money instead of expecting someone else to give it to him. Ten percent of whatever he earned went first to tithe, our family tradition of sharing with others. We did not consider shared family work around the house as work for pay, for any of us; it was considered being part of the community. So he found other projects, usually at our business or selling books at the used bookstore, to raise money. Jim and I often had to halt our instincts to buy for him, because he was so proud of deciding, earning and buying for himself. We gave him more of ourselves, our time, our attention, instead of our money, which is always a good idea.

A book that Michael wanted, saved for, and bought himself meant so much more. And the resulting self-esteem is obvious. We tried to keep quiet when he wanted to spend his earnings on "plastic junk", only asking that he try to donate the same amount of plastic toys that he didn't want anymore to the Salvation Army so the house doesn't fill up with plastic.

Michael was very generous with his money in buying gifts for others or in helping out with groceries or other expenses. We made an effort to keep in mind the categories of his budget and to give him opportunities to help with buying food and clothing, paying for gas, and so forth. I think it made all of us aware of the difference between wanting and needing something, and shopping for necessities instead of for entertainment.

One year while visiting family, his aunt and grandmother offered to buy him a T-shirt. He studied the shirt, checked the price, and announced to everyone's surprise, "I don't need another T-shirt, thank you."

At age ten Michael received $20 a month, and this allowance was never tied to behavior or used as a reward or punishment. There were ten budget categories now, music having been added. He had a notebook-checkbook (a full size ring binder) with ten ledger pages and ten 5" x 7" manila cash envelopes, holes punched to fit in the notebook. This notebook was his favorite Christmas present that year!

With every deposit or withdrawal he kept a record on the appropriate page. We opened savings and checking accounts at our bank for him, and when money in the savings category piled up it went into the bank, Michael keeping track of the interest. We signed the signature card at the bank since he was underage, but he filled out and signed the checks. Checks were only used to pay for music lessons.

Sometimes Michael wanted to spend the money he earned without going through these steps so he decided how much cash to carry. This work was considered real, practical and important life skills, not just a math exercise that would be needed "some day." This made all the difference. He enjoyed getting out his checkbook in stores, sometimes recording the expenditure and doing the math, right at the counter.

Reading this you may get the idea that we spent a lot of time dealing with money. Nothing could be further *from the truth. This system seems to put earning and spending in a proper perspective as a means of making responsible decisions, of contributing, of learning values and not earning and spending a main focus of life.*

Budgeting Time

Because learning about wise and fair spending of money was so much fun and so valuable we started thinking about how our time was spent. We developed a "My Day" chart, adapting it over a period of time. We asked friends, both adults and young people, to fill it out and see how they liked it and if they learned anything of value.

Whole families did this together and found it was very interesting to see who was in charge of what! This introduced "Time Management" in a very interesting way.

Directions for the My Day Chart

1- Record your name and the date. Start at midnight. Fill in how time was/is spent during the day and night.

2- Color-code the activity using the "color key," changing the categories if you see fit (most people consider the time spent filling in this chart as the yellow category "study").

3- At the end of each period fill in the 24-hour squares in the lower right-hand corner.

4- Compare your graph with others, adjust your day and enjoy! Make a completely different chart if you think it would be a better fit for your family.

Since the chart is difficult to see here are color keys

BLUE: helping family or community. Cleaning, working at a job, cooking, etc.

YELLOW: helping oneself, practicing music, studying, writing, attending classes, reading for study, etc.

RED: leisure time, sports, games, reading for fun, TV, parties, hanging out

GREEN: sleeping, bathing, eating, dressing, driving or being driven places, other practical life care of self activities

Algebra

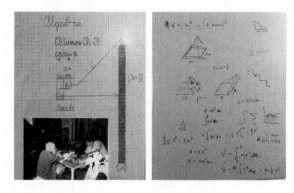

When Narda and her fiancé Ulysses, whom she had met in Africa, as they were both Peace Corps volunteers, returned to the US, they came to visit us. At that time I had two pieces of elementary math/geometry materials that I had no idea how to use. They had not been part of my training and I had bought them at a used toy store hoping to someday figure out what they were for. Ulysses is an engineer so I thought he might be able to help us.

He figured out that one piece of material was for figuring the volume of a prism and the other was a representation of an algebraic formula similar to but larger than the cubes of the binomial and tri-nomial.

The most enjoyable part of this experience was Ulysses, Jim, Michael, Narda, and I sitting around the table working on math and algebra and enjoying it.

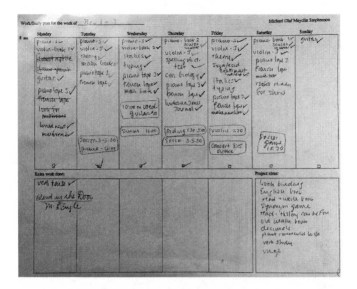

RECORD KEEPING

As Michael now had scheduled lessons and other events outside the home during the week, he developed a new way to keep track of his work. Together we created the above form on the computer and he filled it out weekly.

For example, on Thursday two events are circled because they take place at a specific time outside the house: riding and soccer.

The following assignments for Thursday he recorded when he made the week plan: piano, violin, personal spelling dictionary test, cell biology, piano tape, French tape, Indiana Jones journal (writing about the Young Indiana Jones history episodes). All of these were completed and checked off.

If they had not been completed Michael would have added them to the schedule for the following week. Because he completed everything on the list for Thursday he checked the box at the bottom. If he had done extra work on that day it would have been written in the bottom box for Thursday.

In the "project ideas" box on the lower right hand corner of the page he wrote things he and Jim and I thought would be good to pursue since he had become interested in them. Michael filed these weekly plans in his 5th grade binder.

Journals

In the fifth grade year, when I required a temporary 100-words-a-day writing assignment, Michael began a journal for that purpose. Even though that assignment didn't really work and didn't last long — he did not enjoy being assigned to write and I didn't want to make him dislike writing as had happened before — he wrote in it periodically over the next few years and today it is very interesting to read.

SIXTH GRADE

During my AMI Montessori training it was extremely valuable that we made all of our timelines and charts by hand, took notes by hand, spent many hours measuring, illustrating, and working with the materials, and created our own albums. We could focus on children in the classroom; the charts and materials were in our hands, our minds, and in our hearts—instantly available to us when needed. Because of this I could create a rough sketch of an elementary class chart whenever the illustration would help make an impression during a conversation.

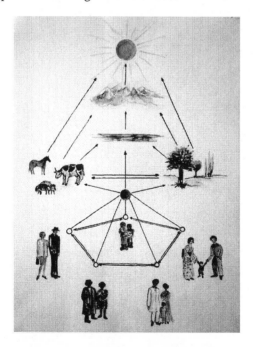

The Chart of Interdependence

The *Chart of Interdependence* is a culmination of the elementary work. It illustrates how all of the areas of study — earth, plants and animals, and humans and their creations — are related and dependent upon each other. The sun is important to the earth; human need plants; plants need healthy soil and ideally organic farming methods; different groups of humans need each other.

With this chart students begin to make sense of the interdependence of all that they have been learning about through the years. Because this presents reality not as *chaos* but as a logical relationship among elements of the cosmos, it is known as a *cosmic vision* or a *cosmic plan*.

The Montessori elementary work has gradually been widened over the years to include an understanding of the fact that all of these interdependencies must be kept in mind to ensure a happy and healthy future for all. Michael was just one of many fortunate young people to be exposed this vision of the meaning of life.

Cosmic Task

During the homeschooling years we continually referred to the fact that each of us has a role to play in this interdependence. This is not only something in the future such as a profession; it is a present role, today, every day. Helping a neighbor, planting vegetables in a healthy way, entertaining others through music. This role in life is called a *cosmic task* in the Montessori world. And searching for this role becomes a habit.

Socialization

Let us return to the first element mentioned at the very beginning of this book, and the first question asked of homeschoolers: *What about socialization?*

Michael continued attending Mistwood once a week, taking music classes on Saturday, and playing sports. Over the years Michael had become comfortable with people of all ages, babies, elementary students, musicians of all ages, adult friends of his sisters, and now he had begun to branch out to learn from professionals.

Learning from the Experts

Through his interest in ancient cultures, exposure to cultures through travel, and reading the Roman history novel *I, Claudius,* Michael began to research preparation for becoming an archeologist. We had told him that it is important in any research to always go to the original sources of the written word rather than paying attention to short quotes, or interpretation by others. We told him to go to the most qualified person possible in researching particular questions.

Michael had become interested in the 1991 discovery of *Otzi, the Iceman* who was found embedded in melting ice of a glacier in the Italian Alps by two hikers. One of the archeologists studying Otsi was Dr. Robert Hedges of the Archaeology Department at Oxford University. Michael mind-mapped archeology and his thoughts about studying this subject and then wrote to Dr. Hedges for advice on how to proceed.

They exchanged long and interesting letters, Dr. Hedges going into fine detail about the field, the necessity of a broad view of humans, developing a logical mind for doing scientific research, and the difference between UK and American archeology. He recommended a book by a colleague at the lab, John Gowlett, *Ascent to Civilization*, and put Michael in touch with a younger colleague at the lab, Christopher Ramsey. Christopher contacted Michael by email and gave Michael book suggestions such as those by Mary Renault written in the 1980's and 1990's.

Sports

Michael continued working to be better at Hwa Rang Do and soccer. Good friends of ours had four tickets to the World Cup game between Cameroon and Brazil to be held at Stanford University. At the last minute they couldn't come so they sent the tickets to Michael. A great experience for Michael, Jim, and two friends they took to the game.

Academics

Jim and I, and now his sisters Narda and Ursula, who had become very supportive of Michael's homeschooling education, suggested and offered experiences, and shared our own interests and passions. We did not pay much attention to what he would have been studying in school.

Archaeology and music were two of many interests that engulfed Michael during this year. His choice was respected and we gave him the tools to find out more. We were not thinking about what Michael would do or be when he was an adult but rather feeding his love of learning and a search for truth.

THE EARTH

Earthquakes

Even before we moved north to Humboldt county Michael had been interested in earthquakes. We had experienced small quakes regularly in the San Francisco Bay Area. Whenever we went into the city of San Francisco we tried to make time to get to the Academy of Sciences in Golden Gate Park.

Michael's favorite experience there was the earthquake simulator. To experience what an earthquake feels like, a few people at a time gathered in a small room with a screen to watch. A narrator described the details of earthquakes in the past as pictures were shown on the screen. The sounds of the fire engines could be heard, and the room began to move in such a way that participants in the exhibit could experience the length of time and the magnitude of an earthquake.

In those days it was the famous 1906 San Francisco Earthquake that was simulated. It occurred at 5:12 am on April 18, 1906, with a magnitude (measurement of the amount of energy released from the event, seismic waves measured by a seismograph) of 7.9 that lasted more than 90 seconds. 90 seconds is a very long time when one is imagining that one is experiencing a real earthquake. I believe that this experience of a simulation was very helpful in preparing us to react calmly when a real earthquake occurred.

More recently this earthquake simulator includes an experience of the Loma Prieta earthquake that our family experienced when we were living in Oakland. It occurred at 5:00 PM on October 17, 1989.

I was standing in our front yard, Jim was at work, and Michael was on the way home from an art class with a friend. The earthquake seemed to go on forever, and I actually heard the collapse of a section of the double-deck freeway not far from our home. It was natural for Michael to want to know more about details of the earth.

In a Montessori elementary, 6-12, class, the older children come to the *great lesson* on the creation of the solar system and the earth that is being given to the new young students at the beginning of each year. These older students now see these events in a new way and begin to understand exactly what is going on at a molecular level, thus moving logically from physics to chemistry.

By sixth grade Michael begin to understand the earlier physics experiments, and newer chemistry experiments, in a new way. They inspired curiosity and a deeper understanding of what had happened when the earth was created, and what was going on now on earth and in the universe.

We did not use a chemistry textbook or workbook, but Michael researched the chemicals and the chemical processes related to his interest. Then he recorded much of this research in his journal to remember it.

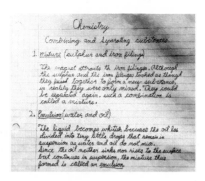

The picture above shows his notes on combining and separating substances - the difference between a mixture (tested with the sulphur and iron fillings experiment), and an emulsion (water and oil).

Experiencing earthquakes must seem a drastic way to learn about the earth, but it certainly can make a person think more about the millions of years when volcanoes and smoke covered the earth. It makes a person think about the changes that have occurred over the years. It brings to mind awareness of the fragility of the planet like no textbook could, and awakens a desire to learn more in order to be able to protect the earth as much as possible.

PLANTS AND ANIMALS

As you must have noticed in this book, there is no way to predict where, when, and how curiosity to know more will begin. It could be something on the cover of a magazine, an overheard conversation, a study being undertaken by another student, or a movie. The Montessori teacher watches for this spark and than offers a way to move forward in learning more.

Now the Guinea worm (Dracunculiasis) disease (GWD), prevalent in West Africa, became an important disease for Michael to learn about. It is caused by simply drinking water containing water fleas that have been infected by a Guinea worm. The larvae migrate to the small intestine of the human body and grow into worms. These worms, reaching up to three feet in length, migrate through the connective tissue and a year later begin to emerge from somewhere on the body. How could such a situation fail to attract the imagination of the elementary child?

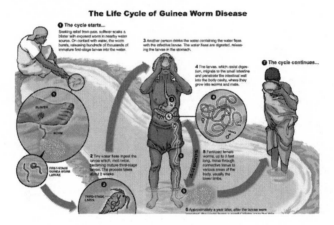

(Picture from cartercenter.org)

Michael's sister Narda at this point had been working through the Peace Corps to help the eradication of the Guinea worm, in Côte d'Ivoire, West Africa, and later worked for the Carter Center on Guinea worm eradication. The disease and Narda's work led to an interest in other particular African diseases which led to watching the movie *Outbreak*, which was partly filmed in Ferndale, California, not so far from where we live. From an email to Michael from Narda

The disease in the movie is called Motaba after the fictional village where it was found in the movie. There isn't a virus named Motaba, but there is one named Ebola. The real disease, Ebola, is named after a river in Central Africa where the virus first started infecting people. It has the same effects on the human body that the movie-version, Motaba, has: bleeding from all the body orifices, flu symptoms, and rapid destruction of the human body. It isn't quite as rapid but it is fast enough

I recommend you read the book The Hot Zone (on which the movie is based). It tells you everything you want to know about the Ebola virus – even about a group of monkeys who were imported to the US and were infected with it. Luckily it didn't mutate to kill humans as it did monkeys, otherwise many people would certainly have died most horrible deaths. I find the disease very fascinating and am considering going to see Outbreak a second time!

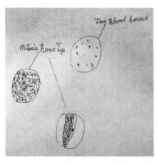
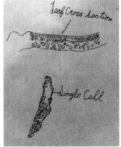

After this intense interest in the human body we purchased a student-quality microscope and Michael prepared cells from plants and hair and skin and began to draw them in his journal.

PEOPLE

Michael continued to spend time with people of all ages, infants through seniors, and to learn about human life from their perspective.

The *Young Indiana Jones* videos from the library last year really inspired Michael to want to learn more about cultures old and new. Because of the success of these videos, books were published that provided more historical information. Here are some that Michael read: *South of the Border* (Mexico), *The Revolution in Russia*, *The Irish Rebellion*, and *The Valley of the Kings* (Egypt).

At the end of the elementary years Michael thought a lot about making the study of cultures his life's work.

After visiting the Oakland Museum, OMCA, Michael wrote quite a bit about what he learned there. This visit was a culmination of so many areas he had been studying over the last year, flora and fauna, geology, migration over the Bering Straits, the gold rush, immigration, political movements including the Vietnam anti-war movement, the environmentalism of John Muir (we had visited his home when in Scotland), the '60s, Silicon Valley. Also, the details were made clear about the name "California', the name given to a mythical island populated by Amazon warriors of the Greek myths (described in a 16th century Spanish novel), and the periods when California was part of "New Spain" and then Mexico. This was an excellent local history and culture field trip for the end of the elementary years.

LANGUAGE

Literature

From Michael's journal:

I have been collecting books from a series of abridged classics for several years. This started when Susan brought five of them home. The first one I ever read was The Strange Case of Dr. Jekyll and Mr. Hyde. Now I have about thirty-seven mostly bought in used bookstores.

One of my favorites is Mutiny on the Bounty, based on a real event, about a ship traveling to the South Pacific, Captain William Bligh is really mean so the crew mutinies. The abridged version is from Bligh's point of view. He thought he was a good person because he followed all of the rules of the British Navy. I think what he wrote about in his ship's log was not what he really thought but what he wanted people to hear. A second book I read was from the point of view of a midshipman, Roger Byam and there is a movie from this point of view.

I think there are lessons to be learned from this story. One is what goes around comes around, and the other is that truth depends on who is telling the story.

Reading abridged classics often inspired Michael to eventually read the original. And being familiar with the plot and characters ahead of time made it easy to become involved with the original classic story.

Also during this time we watched three different video versions of *Hamlet* and it was clear that there were three different ways to interpret the personalities and the roles of both Polonius and his daughter Ophelia. Even though the words spoken were the same, the facial expressions and body language variations gave completely different impressions. This awareness in the videos inspired Michael to read the book.

Latin

Bolchazy-Carducci Publisher's Latin books and tapes were used by many homeschoolers. Personally I know that the logic and intense analysis of language I learned when studying Latin in high school, and tutoring it in college, was very valuable. It is linked to words one encounters everyday, and to the development of language over centuries. I was very glad that Michael was interested in studying Latin. Through these books and tapes he could do it at his own pace.

As I have mentioned before Michael was now attempting to direct his questions to the most knowledgeable person he could find. So one day when he was taking a Latin test and scoring himself at the end he disagreed with the answer. He wrote to the publishers with his thoughts on the matter. I think they must have enjoyed his letter because they wrote a long reply explaining the answer and thanking him for taking the initiative and challenging the Latin when he thought it was wrong.

E-mail

Now Michael was able to communicate with his sisters by email. Ursula was traveling in South America and Narda was in Denver taking the Montessori 0-3 training. Michael shared with them some of what he was learning in Latin and this was Narda's reply:

Did you know that "est" means "to be" or "is" in French too? So in French, "It is a bull" is "C'est un taureau." French is based on Latin. You can send me more simple Latin phrases and I'll translate them into French, then we can see how similar the ancient and modern languages are.

Mindmapping

Mindmapping is an effective way of gathering and connecting information from one's brain. When I am consulting with a school I mindmap every day in order to decide what to share at the closing meeting. When writing a talk or beginning a book I do the same thing.

This the sixth grade year Michael began using this technique in preparing to write anything, or sometimes even just to gather his thoughts on a subject. For example he mindmapped the members of the family, one at a time, in order to look at different aspects of all of us.

When he was preparing to write to Dr. Hedges in Oxford, Michael made two mindmaps — one about the subject of archeology and the second about what he wanted to know about preparing to be an archeologist. He wanted his letter to be as clear as possible and not waste the scientist's time.

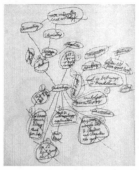 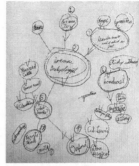

He mindmapped in order to gather his thoughts in writing about the book *Mutiny on the Bounty*. He mindmapped a "thank you" note so that it would be interesting. And mindmapping helped Michael think broadly about a subject he was studying in order to discover what areas he needed to know more about.

Art and Music

During one trip back to the Bay Area, we saw a special exhibit on art through the ages — from prehistoric cultures to the present day — at the Oakland Museum. We also attended a San Francisco Symphony concert and saw the musical *Phantom of the Opera*.

Back at home in Northern California we were very lucky in being able to attract performers that this area could never afford were it not for the case that performers from around the world want to come to see "where the redwood trees meet the ocean." As a result we often were able to see these people mid-week as they are between weekend performances in the San Francisco area, and the Portland or Seattle area.

We usually had two tickets and Jim and I took turns going with Michael, because we thought it most important that he be able to measure his own developing musical ability with the best models possible.

Some of the notable performances from this year included The Gyuto Monks, Throat Singers of Tuva, Dave Brubeck, Ali Akbar Kahn, Alexander String Quartet, Kronos Quartet, Dance Brazil, Momix, American Indian Dance Theatre, and Ladysmith Black Mambazo

MATH AND GEOMETRY
Practical Math

We continued to look for ways to make math relevant and enjoyable, related to today rather than just something one has to slog through day by day in hopes that it will be valuable someday in the future, or the passing of tests being the only goal.

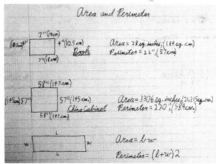

Above are drawings from Michael's journal showing that he measured items in the home, a book and the China cabinet in this picture, and recorded the area of one side. He went on

to measure many items and to figure the volume as well as the area of a side. In his journal:

> *In my budget book I have $55.00 in "toys", and*
> *$1.00 in "books."*

There were not many toys he was interested in at this age, but many good books to save up for.

Geometry

Geometry really captured his attention this year. During my elementary training we began to create our own geometry language materials, pictures, labels, and definitions. Then during teaching I completed over thirty-five different sets for my classroom, including detailed studies of lines, angles, polygons, circles, and triangles. I told Michael the story of a student I had had in an elementary class who loved this material so much that she wanted to make her own set and spent several months doing so. He was inspired.

Michael went through my complete set of booklets, experimented with creating with string, compass, protractor, and colored sticks, and then drew what he had created and the definitions in his journal. Above, showing from two of the booklets, *Two Particular Combinations of Angles* and *Angles Formed by Two Straight Lines*, is only one of many geometry pages in his journal.

Traditional Math

If you look at the one-week record-keeping chart in the next section you will see under "Math" Michael wrote "wordmath" and "fractions". These are workbooks from the teacher's store. Michael worked through them pretty much on his own, with help from us if he needed it.

RECORD KEEPING

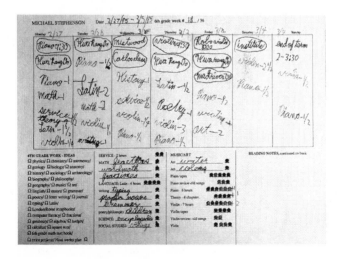

A New Record Keeping System

You can see yet another system of record keeping and time management experimented with this year. The page pictured is from the 18th of 36 weeks of grade six. Now he focused on hours, for example you can see little symbols to fill in to be sure he practiced piano (review of earlier Suzuki pieces 3 hours, listening to Suzuki tapes 5 hours, piano practice of present Suzuki book 6 hours, piano theory 4 chapters.)

In looking through these pages that were filed for this grade I see the following, just some examples of work that has not been mentioned before:

> *service, play music at the senior center, entomology, Vikings, Sim* City [a city-building game, invented by a Montessori graduate and game expert today, and available at the homeschooling school], *Europe map, USA map, mythology, philosophy, concert rehearsal, fractions, cubes, algebra, typing tutor* [typing learned on computer], *National Geographic, Roots* [a favorite book this year], and *The Walton Viola* Concerto [seen during a trip to San Francisco]

Protecting Uninterrupted Concentration

This year there were more outside events scheduled: Hwa Rang Do martial arts, Mistwood homeschooling school on Tuesday, various lessons, and performances.

This sometimes made it difficult for Michael to find time for the many hours a week of silence and uninterrupted time to focus on his work. This is the most important part of Montessori education at any age.

From the very beginning of the kindergarten year Michael had full days of no schedules in order to educate himself. This allowed a continual flow of thinking, moving from one project to another, or taking a break to just curl up and read, have a snack, come to me or Jim for help or a planning meeting for the next week, go outside and swing in the tree swing, or take a nap.

Over the years he had learned that these long periods of uninterrupted concentration, guided by his own inner schedule and interests, and silence to process information and experiences, and just to have time to think, were the most valuable parts of his education and this year it took careful planning to protect them.

END OF ELEMENTARY SCHOOL
Public School Tests

At the end of sixth grade, age twelve, Michael took the Woodcock-Johnson Tests of Achievement given to students in many schools. Here is a rough sketch of the results by grade equivalency. A score 6.9 is end of sixth grade; a score of 12.9 is the end of the senior year of high school:

Language

Word comprehension: 16.8

Passage comprehension: 15.6

Math

Calculation: 7.3

Applied problems: 10.8

> Science: 10.4
>
> Social Studies: 13.1
>
> Humanities: 14.6

Meyers-Briggs Type Indicator Test

Michael also took a Meyers-Briggs Type Indicator Test because a psychologist friend was learning to use this test in her practice. This test, based on the ideas of Jung, indicate different psychological preferences in how people perceive the world and make decisions.

The result of Michael's test showed that he is type INTJ (introversion over extroversion; intuition over sensing; thinking over feeling; judging over perceptive).

Here is a brief explanation of this psychological type:

> *Usually have original minds and great drive for their own ideas and purposes. In fields that appeal to them, they have a fine power to organize a job and carry it through with or without help. Skeptical, critical, independent, determined, often stubborn. Most learn to yield less important points in order to win the most important.*

It was a relief to have these test results as Michael wanted to continue to homeschool and the Montessori ideas for the middle school age include very little in the way of traditionally required academics and far more attention to others ways to learn and grow. So we felt we could go on as close to the Montessori middle school plan as possible.

This year there were more outside events scheduled: Hwa Rang Do martial arts, Mistwood homeschooling school on Tuesday, various lessons, and performances. So it took careful planning to create daily all-important periods of silence and concentration.

THE YOUNG ADULT
7TH to 12th Grades

Maria Montessori was a physician, an anthropologist, a mathematician, an advocate for human rights, and educational reformer. As a result, her perspective on what we call "education" was extremely broad. Her goal, as a scientist was always to learn from observation and testing theories as they become formulated.

In 1947 she inspired the beginning of the Montessori 0-3 program, and in 1948 published the book *From Childhood to Adolescence*, which presents her thoughts on the education of adolescents. All of the quotes in this chapter are from this book.

> *This respect for the children is of the greatest*
> *importance and must be observed in practice. The*
> *adolescent must never be treated as a child, for that is a*
> *stage of life that* [the adolescent] *has surpassed.*

Montessori studied in depth, from the perspective of medicine, anthropology, and human rights, the differences in the needs of humans at different stages of development. It is clear in the image below, which is a simplified version of "the bulb" illustration that Montessori created, that she considered the first three years of life, and the period from twelve to eighteen, to be the time when most physical, mental, and emotional changes take place. These are the periods of life

180

when the most understanding, wisdom, and support is required from the world in order for human beings to thrive.

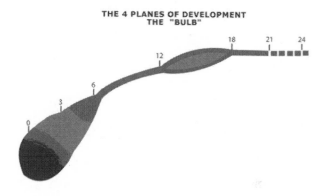

THE 4 PLANES OF DEVELOPMENT
THE "BULB"

The Transition to Adolescence

The time from age six to twelve years is a relatively stable time. This is when the passing on of culture, through the imagination and academic work is easy. Sometimes it is thought, since the years from six to twelve were so successful at taking in academic information that this will continue during the adolescent years. Nothing could be further from the truth.

The years from birth to three lay the foundation for childhood; the years from twelve to eighteen lay the foundation for adulthood.

When the needs of the two-year-old are not met, we observe "the terrible twos". When the needs of the adolescent are not met we can see something similar, a separation of these young adults from family and society because they are not understood, and are not helped to understand themselves.

Written in 1948 and true today:

Everything that concerns education assumes today an importance of a general kind, and must represent a protection and a practical aid to the development of [humans]; *that is to say, it must aim at improving the individual in order to improve society.*

But, above all it is the education of adolescents that is important, because adolescence is the time when the child enters on the state of [adulthood] *and becomes a member of society.*

If puberty is, on the physical side, a transition from an infantile to an adult state, there is also, on the psychological side, a transition from the child to the adult who has to live in society. These two needs of the adolescent: for protection during the time of the difficult physical transition, and for an understanding of the society which [the adolescent] *is about to enter to play* [the adolescent's] *part as an adult, give rise to two problems that are of equal importance concerning education at this age.*

Education should not limit itself to seeking new methods for a mostly arid transmission of knowledge: its aim must be to give the necessary aid to human development.

—Montessori, *From Childhood to Adolescence*

Fulfilled Adolescents in Ohio and Kathmandu

Some years ago I met, and was very impressed with the maturity of, two different groups of adolescents. One consisted of three students from the Montessori *Erdkinder*, or farm school, in Ohio. They were participating in a Montessori birth-three workshop I was giving at a conference in Portland, Oregon.

The other group were students living and studying in a boarding school for indigent village children in Kathmandu, Nepal. I spent a week at the Nepal school, attending classes and sharing meals and conversations with the teachers and students in order to see what Montessori ideas they could make use of.

These two groups of students had a lot in common. They all spoke to me with respect and confidence as though I were their equal. There was no feeling of competition among them to impress the teacher. They listened to each other carefully and with respect. They spoke on a wide range of subjects that had nothing to do with academic studies, but more about the condition of the world and how they could grow into adults who would be able to contribute as responsible and caring citizens.

What did they have in common? They all had experienced an emphasis on practical life work for this stage of development over a standard academic curriculum as the center of their life.

The Ohio students had attended a developing Montessori *Erdkinder* or farm school based on the ideas of Montessori for this age. They were used to real valuable physical work, responsibility, social contribution, working together to solve problems, and being treated as adults by the house parents and teacher.

The school in Nepal existed solely on donations for food and teacher salaries because the students were from extremely poor villages that had no post office, school, medical care, and so on. When I would ask one of the students how far away was their village he or she usually said something like this, "one day by bus, five days walking."

Because of their dire economics the students, between 250-300 at any one time, from age kindergarten through high school, took care of each other and fulfilled many of the roles that would have been taken by adults had there been more money. They cleaned, helped with the cooking, serving, washing up. The adolescents took turns assisting the visiting medics and as they became more adept were able to assist the annual free dental clinic given by dentists by sterilizing the equipment, registering and recording the results of students seeing the dentist, and giving lessons on brushing teeth.

Both groups had academic classes, but these were secondary. For the Ohio students they followed an interest of an individual student as much as possible. And for the Nepal students traditional academic lessons were given only during a few hours each weekday because there was so much to be done just to live and care for each other.

In both groups there was a marked feeling of self-respect that had come from respect for their independence and ability to contribute to society.

> *Overemphasis on the competitive system and premature specialization on the ground of immediate usefulness kill the spirit on which all cultural life depends, specialized knowledge included.*
>
> *It is also vital to a valuable education that independent critical thinking be developed in the young human being, a development that is greatly jeopardized by overburdening him with too much and with too varied subjects . . . Overburdening necessarily leads to superficiality. Teaching should be such that what is offered is perceived as a valuable gift and not as a hard duty.*
>
> —Albert Einstein, "Education for Independent Thought"
> New York Times, Oct. 5, 1952

Showing Respect with Our Words

As a school consultant I often find myself talking about how to truly show respect to students. We of course know to respect concentration by not interrupting it, and to respect a child's choice of work by not judging or preventing if it is suited to their stage of development; but there is more.

We are models first and foremost and our body language, our voice, our words, express how much we truly respect and believe in a student.

Dr. Silvana Montanaro, during our 0-3 Montessori teacher training, enlightened us all in this aspect of true respect when she modeled talking to an infant with the same pitch, vocabulary, and seriousness, as she would use in talking to any of us.

By 1993 I had been teaching and working with children from age two through the high school for many years. I was approached by two Montessori teachers in Portland, Oregon who wanted to pick my brain about their elementary and middle school teaching practice.

Maggie and Kathy and I spent several days together in our home. On the last day we spoke about how to guide children while showing respect. I knew, as I heard them talk about their classes that they were speaking to students with a different voice than they would use in speaking to peers. I wanted to help them understand how being talked to in this way feels.

We were seated at a picnic table in our yard. I asked both teachers to stand next to each other on the deck against the wall of the house. Then I spoke to them the way my teachers might have spoken to me in traditional school when I was growing up, and unfortunately the way I still hear some Montessori teachers speak to students at times. They stood next to each other, waiting.

I stood next to the picnic table with my arms crossed in front of me and with a serious (teachery) expression on my face. But still using a polite voice I said:

We are going to walk down the hall. Please stand in line.

Stand still.

Kathy put your hands by your side.

Maggie, no talking. Did you hear me?

I'll wait here until everyone is ready.

Maggie looked shocked, and then she slumped forward and called out, "Stop Susan, I get it! "

I asked them if they felt that I was respecting them. Kathy replied, "It felt so belittling and controlling."

Here is another example. Years ago I was studying French at *Alliance Française* in Paris. Over lunch we students sometimes could visit with our teachers, laughing together at our attempts at rudimentary French. After lunch we returned to the classroom. The teacher entered the room and closed the door and transformed into the boss who held all the knowledge, which would be forced on us according to her schedule and directions. I know this is tradition in many places but it is not the kind of education that makes a person feel respected, excited, and inspired to want to learn more.

This kind of "talking down" to a person is embarrassing to adults, and it should not be something that our adolescents are used to. I cringe when I hear even the nicest Montessori teachers speaking this way to children at any age. There is a better way.

When I was writing this chapter I reached out to Maggie and Kathy, both still Montessori teachers, to find out if there were things they had changed after our discussion about showing respect through our words. Here is what Kathy wrote:

> For me it changed my way of relating to students. I starting talking to them as I would another older person and trying to interest them in things the way I would another peer. I would say, "I read an interesting book about Lewis and Clark and was fascinated by . . ." And next thing the child was interested too. It helped me watch for and pull out their interests.
>
> It also changed the way of talking to students when they were being too loud, for example. I recall being out to dinner with my parents once and becoming loud and excited until finally a waitress came over and said, "Sorry but your table is being loud and that table said they are having a hard time hearing each other talk." Everyone laughed and we quieted down. The waitress didn't come over and say, "You are being too loud; you need to be quiet. Or you will have to separate. This is one warning..." Your example came to mind.
>
> I began to see how ridiculous it was to talk to people like that. If I said, "We are doing some work over here and can't hear each other because it is loud" the students would fix it without my saying anything else.
>
> Yours was a life-shifting lesson for me. And has allowed me to have good relations with young people over the years.

I know that we parents and teachers are not perfect. It is natural, when finding ourselves in a situation with our children or students where we don't have the immediate access to the perfect response, to revert to our own educational experience, to speak the way we were spoken to as children or students.

Montessori parenting and teaching is a life-long voyage of learning how to understand the needs of others and of ourselves; we learn to observe ourselves and the situation, to pause and gather our thoughts, and to respond intelligently, lovingly, and with respect.

Adolescent Teacher Montessori Certification

For many years there have been Montessori adolescent (age 12-18) education experiments in several countries, both in the countryside and in cities. The goal is to meet the physical, emotional, and mental needs of this age. As of this year there is even a program where adults can take this training and receive an AMI (Association Montessori Internationale) certification.

This is a very important movement that will teach us all about what students from age twelve and older need to thrive, and to be happy, responsible, compassionate, hardworking, creative, individuals.

But very few families and individuals are able to participate in these experiments because of distance and money and availability of programs. I am sure that there are many young adults who have never heard of Montessori who are positive and happy and becoming well-educated individuals. In wondering what they might have in common I think it is likely that many have been able to use their minds and hands functioning together toward an intelligent purpose as is the goal in Montessori at all ages. They have been able to make mistakes without grades or judgment, and to fix them. They have learned to adapt to the needs of their group.

> *The world is partly in a state of disintegration and partly in a state of reconstruction. Adaptability – this is the most essential quality; for the progress of the world is continually opening new careers, and at the same time closing or revolutionizing the traditional types of employment. This does not mean that in secondary schools there should be no preparation for the intellectual professions . . . but* [people] *with hands and no head, and* [people] *with head and no hands are equally out of place in the modern community*

Physical Needs of the Adolescent

In *From Childhood to Adolescence*, Montessori gives quite a few examples of physical needs for this age. For example because the body is growing quickly the young adult often needs a lot of sleep. In our culture today students are kept so busy with traditional school requirements that the only time they have to communicate with each other about life is late at night, which means more need for sleep.

She also speaks of the importance of fresh and nutritious food, clean air, life in the open air and sunshine, and long walks.

Mental and Psychological Needs of the Adolescent

The impulse to be important, to be valuable to society, and do real work, puts the Montessori concept of *practical life work* at the top of the list of needs at this age. And if these efforts can result in some level of economic independence this is even better.

Adolescents need to be creative, to come up with their own ideas, to test theories, and to feel that they are contributing members of society.

The chief symptom of adolescence is a state of expectation, a tendency towards creative work and a need for the strengthening of self-confidence.

The stress of academic work all day, homework at night, and free time spent on screens is physically, mentally, and emotionally unhealthy and overwhelms young adults. Life is better when manual work, academic work, and physical rest are balanced and one has the time to process and think for oneself. In such a more healthy situation there is a chance that a young person will not be programed by society as to what to think, who to be, what to look like, what life is all about. Such a young person will learn to think independently and to grow in wisdom and understanding. Such intellectual freedom can lead to unexpected and exciting examples of creativity.

Some Creative Young Adults

Throughout history, and today, young adults have made and are making their mark. At age 15 Greta Thunberg of Sweden began an environmental movement that has spread around the world. At age 11 Malala Yousafzai in Pakistan began fighting for girls' rights to education and by age 17 became the youngest winner of the Nobel Peace Prize. At age 16, Alexander the Great, having just finished studying under Aristotle, was the regent in charge of Macedonia. The American Jordan Romero climbed Mt. Everest at Age 13. William Cullen Bryant published his first poem at age 10. The great French thinker Blaise Pascal began studying geometry at age 12 and was soon recreating the geometry theories of Euclid. Picasso, it is said, at age 12 drew like Raphael. Felix Mendelsson wrote his first composition when he was 11. Jean Piaget, a Swiss follower of Montessori, talked his way into a job at the local Museum of Natural History at the age of 10. Enrico Fermi by age 10 was mulling over geometric proofs and building electric motors; Clara Schumann began composing her own pieces at 10, and made her concert debut at the age of 11. At age 13 Joan of Arc led the French army in a major victory against the English. At 15 Bobby Fischer became the youngest chess player in history to be named grandmaster, and Louis Braille developed the alphabet for the blind when he was just 15 years old.

It is doubtful if most of these inventions, or these accomplishments, would have occurred if the time and energy of these children and young adults had been taken up by purely academic pursuits, the subject and schedule decided on by a central government.

Montessori Homeschooling, One Family's Story

I will share ways that our family collaborated — all family members together — to learn more and more how to meet the physical, mental, psychological needs during the middle school homeschooling years. I hope that our stories will be helpful to other parents and to teachers as they get to know their young people, to observe their interests, and meet their needs.

SEVENTH GRADE

PHYSICAL NEEDS

Sleep

It was clear that Michael needed more sleep beginning this year. But that was not a problem. For all of the homeschooling years it was up to each member of the family to decide when to go to sleep at night and when to get up in the morning. And as we learn in the Montessori 0-3 training, an idea supported by science today, it is important to avoid waking a sleeping person except in an emergency.

Food and Environment

We are fortunate to have a food co-op in town and to live in a place where the air is clean and it is possible to walk on a usually deserted beach (we are in a cold area where surfers wear wetsuits all year long) and in the woods. On river trips with his sister Ursula and her friends and clients he spent time in pristine areas of California and Oregon and slept out under the stars.

Exercise

In sixth grade Michael was still quite serious about the martial art of Hwa Rang Do and kept a journal with copious notes of the philosophy and the moves he was working on, but at the end of the year he wrote a very polite letter to the sensei explaining that he was a bit overwhelmed with work and planning to take a break. It was clear that the adolescent rapid growth requiring rest was setting in.

Michael still got plenty of exercise doing real work, hauling boxes when he was working at the Michael Olaf store, and stacking and bringing in firewood at home.

The work helping his sister on river-rafting trips was strenuous but balanced with plenty of quiet restful time, on the river and the shore.

PSYCHOLOGICAL NEEDS

Joy, feeling one's own value, being appreciated and loved by others, feeling useful and capable of production are all factors of enormous value for the human soul.
— Montessori, *From Childhood to Adolescence*

Groups

Being a successful, respected, and contributing member of a group is very important at this age. And the family is the primary group to be considered. One of the most valuable parts of homeschooling was the time we were able to spend together, Jim and Michael and me, and sometimes Michael's sisters, and later their families. We learned a lot about each other and it was always possible to take time to talk—now as equals—about politics, nature, the arts, the news, plans, work, all the things that young adults benefit from discussing with their families.

There were other important groups in Michael's life this year. These were the homeschooling school, Mistwood Center for Education, where Michael went once a week. In the picture above the seventh and eighth graders don their costumes for a play and the next day would head to Ashland, Oregon for the annual trip to the Oregon Shakespeare Festival.

At Mistwood all of the students, from kindergarten through eighth grade were in the same environment, all learning to consider and take care of each other. By seventh grade there was a lot of practice in helping and teaching and caring for the young.

One of the projects at Mistwood was for students to write a few words about what they appreciated about each other. Each student ended up with a small book, a Christmas gift, made up of the comments. Here is what his friends thought of Michael:

> *Funny, cool, good at making people laugh, good at magic* (a game he still plays in this thirties), *a good sense of humor, a good person, can tell good jokes, kind of silly, you include people in games, you have a good temper, you play the piano expressively and you are a good actor, you have a good sense of humor, you are good at math and soccer and capture the flag and four square, you make very funny jokes*

Music Groups

I would put music ensembles in a special category when thinking about learning to function in a group. There are many skills that come into play. One person does not stand out but must listen to all of the others and play at a volume that makes the music valuable. One must practice so as not to hold others back during a rehearsal and at the same time must develop patience when others have not practiced enough and need additional help. One must listen to the conductor and do what the conductor requires, learning to obey for the good of the group and the music. A large ensemble will break into smaller sectional groups; all string players together for an example, for practice. The same skills apply here as well but there is the added benefit of acting as part of a small group, giving and taking feedback, solving musical problems with good manners and consideration for others.

Real Work – Planning a House

We use the term *valorization* to describe young adults who, through work, become aware of the fact that their ideas and their efforts are important and necessary to the group; they have value. Michael was daily a contributing member of our family; his ideas and his work was indeed valuable.

This year we decided it was time to build a house, finally to own a house instead of renting. We researched straw bale construction but realized that we would need a bank loan in order to buy land and build, so that plan was not approved. Through friends we found a local contractor to help us.

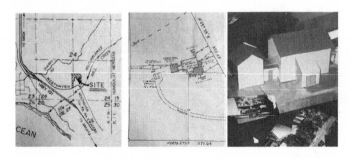

Michael was involved with every step as we looked at the family finances to see what we could afford if we did a lot of the work ourselves, made a budget, put up home-made lovely posters to notify people what we were looking for ("classical musicians looking for a quiet piece of earth"), found a piece of land, made appointments at the county offices to see the boundaries and find out the rules about land and buildings, drew the plot plan ourselves, drew the house plans on squared paper and made a model of what we hoped the house would look like.

Real Work at the Family Business

In our small family business there were endless possibilities for Michael to participate in real work. I created the catalog for our Michael Olaf Montessori Company on the home computer so Michael began to learn to use the computer programs (Word, InDesign/PageMaker, Photoshop). He was acutely aware of the time involved and that a need for his help was real and necessary, proofreading and testing books and products. He went along to the printing company to see the film being developed and then to the giant newspaper printing company in another city to see the catalog be printed and to check the color in the first run of covers, and adapting percentages of colors till the cover looked right.

At work with Jim, Michael did quite a bit of work on the mailing of catalogs, removing duplicates from the computer mailing list, labeling, sorting by zip code, bundling in the correct number of books per bundle, and carrying the bags to the post office with Jim.

Michael still got a small amount for monthly allowance but as he could see where the money for our rent and food came from he was, from this early age, quite aware of the value of money and its relationship to work. We only had one or two employees so sometimes he earned extra money for work that really needed to be done by him.

MENTAL NEEDS
Academic Choices – Following Interests

Michael continued to be interested in world cultures. As he was preparing to leave for a trip to Colorado for his sister's wedding, and then a volunteer trip to Peru with a family who provided free dental work to groups of indigent people around the world, he wrote again to Dr. Hedges the Archaeologist at Oxford for suggestions to prepare to learn more in the world of archeology.

Dr. Hedges wrote that he had been to Mesa Verde when working for a year in Colorado and recommended a visit. He said he was envious that Michael would be able to visit Machu Picchu, in his words, "perhaps the most dramatic of any archaeological site anywhere."

Even though Dr. Hedge's advice was that it is better to read up on a place visited after the trip, he shared a lot of information about the Incas and suggestions for what to look for in both Colorado and Peru. He suggested articles in *Scientific American*, George Bankes' *Peru before Pizarro*, and

Hans Li's *The Ancient Ones* in preparation. He warned Michael to be critical when reading the ideas of people like Von Daniken (Michael had told him that he was reading these books).

After Narda's wedding in Denver we drove all the way across the state to explore Mesa Verde and Michael kept a detailed record of what he learned about the Anasazi from our Navajo and Hopi guides.

The parents of Michael's friend Tyler were very experienced travelers and medical volunteers and they included both boys in their work and in learning as much about Peru as possible. In the mountains they provided free dental work to the indigent Indians, Michael and Tyler taking care of the children while the adults had their teeth worked on. Then together they explored the ancient Inca city Machu Picchu and walked the Inca trail. After the work was finished they traveled to Lima and visited the museums and other historical and cultural sights of Peru.

Before they left for South America I had created a research guide for both boys, asking them to find the answers before, during, or after the trip, and then to share them with their friends at the homeschooling school.

The questions touched upon the history of South America and of Peru, geologic plates, natural resources, animals, musical instruments (drawings of both animals and musical instruments), politics, ancient cultures, geographic regions, Machu Picchu discovery, and questions about how the country could be improved. They had to find translations of some important words (in Quechua and Spanish). The last question was, "What questions would you include, or leave out, for friends planning a trip to Peru?"

Books

In the earlier years of homeschooling we had had a children's animal encyclopedia set, but now we were often referring to an adult set of encyclopedias. Also we added the 51-volume set of *Harvard Classics*, as they were very easy to obtain in a used bookstore. Today it is easy for a person to Google to find out the answers to any question, but it has been proven that when one looks through a print book to find the answer there is much greater chance for the information to remain. When one gets a quick answer on the Internet it disappears from our minds almost as quickly as it is obtained.

The set of Harvard Classics were very helpful because it began the practice of getting information from original writings or speeches instead of relying on portions selected by others, especially for news headlines. Although most of the works are from Western Civilization there were a few references to religions of Buddhism, Hinduism, Judaism, and Islam. It was so valuable to have at our fingertips essays by physicists, politicians, and philosophers, poetry, works such as *The Divine Comedy, The Origin of the Species, Voyage of the Beagle,* and the original folklore and children's tales by Anderson and Aesop.

Creativity - Writing

Michael was still attending the homeschooling school one day a week. There were no formal classes but the writing suggestions were clearly doing a better job of getting Michael to write than mine were! Here is an example:

Hooked

By Michael Stephenson, 1/1996

Bright sunlight sifted through the branches above me. It was a very warm day and I could hear birds singing in the trees around me. It was a perfect day, but I was hungry. I walked over to where my servants had put out my daily food supply. I smelled that lovely aroma and dug in.

I was halfway through my feast when I heard a growl behind me. I turned around and saw my arch nemesis standing there growling, saliva was dripping off her tongue which was hanging out of her mouth at a weird angle. She started to sniff my food.

I did not stop her; no reason to get in a fight I thought. But what she did made me boil. She stopped sniffing and scooped up several treats with her long tongue. I couldn't stand it. I hissed, thrusting my claws deep into her snout. I pulled back to strike again but my claws were stuck in her nose. She started to nip at my face so I struck at her with my free claws but then they too got hooked into her face. I struggled and struggled but it was no use. The situation was looking hopeless until one of my

203

servants came, calmed us both down, and gently unhooked my claws.

Slowly the drooling canine walked away as I finished my feast.

Creativity - Music

Michael continued studying and performing music, playing viola, percussion, and piano in several concerts with the junior orchestra and chamber ensemble at the music academy. Michael and I played a duet (Michael on violin, I on piano) *Hungarian Dance no. 5* by Brahms at a recital and in a concert given by The Music Teachers Association of California he played *Minstrels from Prelude*, a piano solo by Debussy. He also performed Mozart's *Ah vous dirai-je, Maman* (variations on Twinkle, Twinkle, Little Star).

I had performed and competed as a pianist through my senior year in high school but Michael had now officially surpassed me in piano mastery and performance—the Montessori way! For a Christmas gift for family and friends Michael made a music tape of his favorite pieces on several instruments.

In second semester at the music academy Michael took a steel pan (steel drums) class and joined the percussion ensemble. By the end of the year, after attending an HSU (Humboldt State University) Percussion Ensemble Concert, he became very interested in steel drums and Latin music.

Since he didn't have a steel drum Michael made flat outlines out of two large pieces of cardboard—the different notes clearly delineated — and spread them out on the kitchen table to practice. They looked very much like the image here.

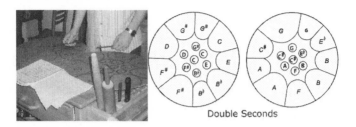

Double Seconds

This inspired him to work more at Michael Olaf and save money so he could buy his own steel drum.

Creativity - Drama

The two women who ran the homeschooling school really enjoyed drama and so at least one group of students were always working on a play. Michael performed in Romeo and Juliet.

One of the essays he wrote was about the play he and friends were in in Scotland, *Fuenteovejuna*. He was glad to be able to share the details of this experience with friends who would know what it felt like to have performed the play eight times in two weeks and then given a performance at a men's prison in Cambridge.

Academic Classes

Michael continued to have occasional French, science, math, history, geography, at the homeschooling school, but about two hours a week at the most.

For several years now we had made weekly trips to the public library and came home with a stack of books. Most of these were non-fiction, subjects that Michael had become interested in, but the pile grew larger as he looked through the library shelves. Fiction books he enjoyed this year included Gene Stratton Porter books (a naturalist who wrote about the area of Indiana where I grew up) and *The Lord of the Rings Trilogy*.

Record keeping was very much like the weekly planning charts that Michael created in sixth grade with the addition of two categories: *family work* and *community service*. Here are some of the items listed: *fractions, poetry, algebra, adjectives, Latin, computer science, bones, gangs, decimals, music composition, build a bird feeder, think, play chess, soccer, tennis, creative writing, library, music at homeless shelter.*

EIGHTH GRADE

PHYSICAL NEEDS

From Michael's journal:

September 12. Today escrow cleared on our new land. Now we own two and a half acres near Trinidad, California. On part of our land where our road is going to be there was a wood and barbed wire fence that Jim and I took down with a wire cutter and our hands.

September 14. Today Jim, Susan, and I hammered stakes into the ground to mark the property line. I am extremely happy at the prospect of having a bigger room in a new house.

Although Michael still occasionally played soccer and went surfing, he had all of the physical work he could handle with the house building. Jim and Michael donned masks and did all of the insulating, and then finishing floors and painting. When the house was finished a friend helped us get loads of rock from the local quarry. The rocks were carried in a wheelbarrow, one at a time for the largest ones, to build retaining walls for the garden,

From Michael's Journal:

September 21: We have some friends that live in Sweden. Their names are Monika and Sune; their kids' names are Stefan and Andrea. Mom is in San Francisco picking up Stefan. He is coming to live with us for about a year.

Stefan had been adopted from Peru when he was very young. A few years earlier Stefan and his family had visited us and we learned that because of his dark skin Stefan was being exposed to a new prejudice in Sweden. We invited him to come and live with us. At the beginning of this year we received a phone call saying that he was ready to come!

Stefan became a member of the family and a brother to Michael. He was very strong and gifted with mechanical and practical information, so he helped us a lot with building the house. He joined Jim and Michael installing insulation and shoveled mud with Michael and me as it was washing into the house from the hill behind us, before a French drain was dug.

Stefan loved the fact that our neighbors were from Mexico, China, Russia, and the USA, and that in our neighborhood there were both college professors and back-to-the land hippies.

He was happy to learn about Peru from me, and at Halloween to wear a Peruvian hat, carry an Andean panpipe, and wrap himself in a Peruvian blanket, all brought back from Lima. He no longer felt different.

Stefan was a good cook and was used to healthy foods as we were. He attended Mistwood, the homeschooling school, with Michael even though he was two years older. And after school and on non-school days both of them surfed, hiked, and rode bikes. I am sure Michael became physically stronger this year because of this new friend.

PSYCHOLOGICAL NEEDS

Groups

Michael played in more music ensembles this year, including a new small local orchestra, The Mad River Philharmonic, that was composed of local string players and one pianist. Once a week we gathered in the Trinidad church/library, moved the library shelves out of the way and set up chairs, and read music. We rarely performed but it was a lot of fun and helped improve our playing. Jim and Michael played violin and I played viola. My stand partner (we shared the same music stand) was Charles Fulkerson, music professor emeritus from the university who was a famous pianist and orchestra leader and, after retirement, decided to learn to play the viola.

Michael and Stefan shared many friends of all ages at Mistwood homeschooling school, and Stefan was in a rock band with Michael this year.

Cooperation vs. Competition

For years at our store we had carried the non-competitive, cooperative games invented and manufactured by a family in Ontario, Canada.

I still remember the first time I played their game called *Harvest Time*. The board contained spaces for four vegetable gardens. One to four persons could play. First a player threw one of the dice and drew a card. Then, depending on the card drawn, either placed a *vegetable card* on their "garden" (which meant that a vegetable had been harvested) or placed a *snow card* on their "garden" (which meant that vegetables could not be harvested during that turn because winter was coming.)

In a competitive game the player who filled his "garden" with vegetables first would win. But with this game, when a person filled their "garden" with vegetable cards the next turn is used to help a friend harvest. The struggle was against weather, not against another person. The goal was for everyone to help each other get everything harvested before bad weather prevented them from doing so.

I still remember the thrill of happiness I felt watching children play this game and help each other for the first time.

The *Family Pastimes* family published a book to help people turn any game into a cooperative rather than a competitive game. And their *Co-op Sports Manual* taught how to make any sports activity cooperative.

There is now a Montessori movement to change sports in a similar way, using different kinds of individual and small group, non-competitive, activities to develop sports skills, and changing the rules for football and other team sports to be child-centered, meaning that everyone gets to play, not just the great players who would make the team win.

There were three computers at the Mistwood school and the only games on them were non-competitive games such as Oregon Trails and the community-building Sim City (Sim City was invented by a Montessori graduate.) The atmosphere at the school: the younger children (including kindergarten) being taken care of and included with the games and work of the older (through eighth grade), was similar to that of a Montessori school, preparing children to think about the needs of others and looking for ways to be helpful.

Fair Government

A professor of political science from the university taught a class at Mistwood on civic responsibility and civic literacy. He inspired the older students to become involved with social movements, and to put on bake sales to raise money and get signatures for petitions to help worthy social causes.

During this time we bought a 3-volume set of high school texts on the US political system at a used bookstore. Each volume went into the history of political systems and the creation and function of one of the three governing bodies in the US that were created to ensure a balance of power: the executive branch, congress, and the supreme court.

As to the need for working within social groups, which is often considered important at this age, I would say that Michael's ideas of healthy relationships within groups began with the playing of non-competitive, co-op, games. He went on to explore truth and justice, the rule of law, all of the elements of society that are so important during the young adult years and beyond.

Real Work – Building a House

Every person in the family was considered equal in doing the work of building a house. There was no question that everything Michael was doing with the house-building project was essential. He didn't have time to earn extra money at the family business this year because of building a house and going to Mistwood more often with Stefan. In his budget much of what he received for his monthly allowance, at his own insistence, went to house-building expenses.

MENTAL NEEDS
European History and Culture

Our good friend Geri Walther, the principle violist in the San Francisco Symphony Orchestra, had looked into taking Argenta, her oldest daughter who was one of Michael's best friends, along on a three-week Symphony tour of Europe. The orchestra would be performing in New York, London, Manchester, Amsterdam, Brussels, Paris, Cologne, Dusseldorf, Hamburg, Berlin, Vienna, Munich, and Stuttgart.

Together we figured out that, for the cost of taking a non-performing family member on the European tour, we could get flights for Argenta, Michael, and me, from California to several of the cities where the orchestra were playing, and where I had friends we could visit. We would meet up with Geri and the orchestra, and explore the cities with my friends.

Argenta, also a Montessori student, was interested in the same kinds of exploration as we were — two and a half weeks of learning about the history and culture of the countries where we would be.

In Amsterdam we stayed with old friends — Heidi is now a Montessori teacher trainer — and met up with Geri for a meal in Heidi's home. There were no tulips this time of year, but we enjoyed the museums and a boat trip. The highlight was a visit to the museum in Anne Frank's house because Anne had also attended a Montessori school.

In none of the places could we afford the tickets to see the orchestra perform, but in Amsterdam we were allowed to attend a rehearsal at the Concertgebouw. We saw a wonderful concert including the Tchaikovsky Violin Concerto with soloist Anne-Sophie Mutter.

In Berlin we stayed with an old acting partner of Jim's who is married to a German actress. Paul was wonderful at answering all of the questions about what Berlin was now like, after the fall of the Berlin Wall, showing us all of the pictures and artifacts at the Checkpoint Charlie museum where people tried to escape from East Berlin. Back at their apartment Michael and Paul continued discussions as they played chess. Paul and his wife have lived in East Berlin for many years and traveled a lot so they were a wealth of information. Paul especially knew what two young Americans would like to learn about.

Everywhere we went we were able to pay attention to being good guests, learning how to squeeze ourselves into a corner of a room on the floor to sleep in most cases, keeping our belongings compact and hanging up towels before leaving the bathroom. Michael and Argenta learned how to do laundry and hang it up in front of the heater, how to shop and cook, help with the housework, and adapt to daily life in each of the places where we stayed.

In London we stayed with a good friend Colin, an actor who each summer taught acting at the Suzuki Summer Academy back home. You can see by the picture that the highlight in London for animal-loving Michael (even more than seeing the old Shakespeare theatre, discussing Hamlet's "to be or not to be" soliloquy with two actors while being allowed to hold the skull, and the art galleries) was to have a flock of birds perch on his head, shoulders, arms in Trafalgar Square. It must have brought back memories to the "save the birds" scene in the Mary Poppins movie.

In Vienna we stayed with a young Swiss woman, Andrea, who had taken the Montessori 0-3 training in London with Michael's sister Narda. Andrea had visited us in California, and was now studying psychology in Vienna. During our visit she took us to the Turkish street market to get a taste of the Middle East and to purchase bread and cheese and *kirshwasser* to make us an authentic Swiss fondue; she loved having an excuse to prepare her favorite dish.

The artist we studied (I had suggested focusing on one artist in each city) was Gustav Klimt. We saw the famous painting *The Kiss* at the Belvedere Palace & Art Museum.

In Paris we stayed with Yoko, a violinist friend of Geri's from Japan. Yoko loved talking music with Michael and Argenta and told them about the days when she was at the conservatory in Japan and they all waited excitedly for the next Beatles song to be released because even the classical musicians thought they were geniuses in their originality. It was very cold in Paris so we didn't do anything outside but I was very happy to share the work of my favorite artists, the impressionists at the Musée d'Orsay, and to see the Mona Lisa at the Louvre.

The practice of *going out* (beyond the classroom) is considered an important part of Montessori education from age six or seven on. As I look back I can see how lucky Michael has been to see so much of the world, and this symphony trip was an exceptional experience.

Studying Back at Home

Michael continued to chart his own path in academic inquiry. This year he asked for a subscription to *National Geographic* for his Christmas present. The Europe trip made him want to know more about the world.

He still kept a weekly work plan but this year he needed a separate list to keep up with classical piano practice, rehearsals, and performances, because he was also studying jazz piano, violin, voice, steel drums, and music composition.

One day, on a return trip from San Francisco to Trinidad, the road was very close to Michael's old school, Marin Montessori, so we stopped. The teacher and my friend Phyllis wasn't there but the assistant was happy for Michael to play the piano for the elementary students. After playing she asked him to talk about music. He really held the attention of the young children (having been one himself not so long ago) with music details, and then answered questions. One of the children asked him if he was forced to practice piano as he was growing up. He said, "My mother sat with me to help me practice at first and sometimes she made me practice. But I am very glad she did because eventually I loved to practice and get better."

At the end of eighth grade all of the students at Mistwood took the Stanford Achievement test. Michael scored average or above average in all categories even though he had no idea what this test would cover and had not been "taught to the test."

The Holocaust

There were two things that stayed with Michael after the Symphony tour of Europe and he wanted to continue to study and learn more about them. These were the Checkpoint Charlie museum of the history of the Berlin wall, and Anne Frank's house in Amsterdam.

Jim, forever a serious student of history, could explain the rise of Hitler, World War Two, and the situation in post-war

Europe, leading to the division of Germany into four zones, and the capital, Berlin, also into four zones. Paul had explained the reason for the Berlin wall and for it's coming down as we made our way through the museum taking hours to look at and read everything about trying to escape to West Germany, and the musicians playing as the wall was finally breached.

But Michael's main questions were about how human beings could treat each other in the ways he had seen and heard about up close when in Amsterdam and Berlin. He wanted to understand how people could stand by and let such things happen.

First he checked the book *The Rise and Fall of the Third Reich* out of the library and began reading it and discussing it with us. This book is well written by an American journalist who covered this part of the world for many years. But it did not answer Michael's questions.

A friend of Jim's told us about his colleague in the sociology department at the local university, whose family had all been killed by Nazis and who, at age twelve, had escaped. As an adult his life's work had become an attempt to understand why some people would automatically and instantly, without thinking and while putting their own lives at risk, help another person, often someone they had never met before.

His wife, a professor in the education department, was at the same time researching why altruism or kindness or compassion was not part of the American education curriculum. Together they contributed a lot to the study of altruism. They secured a grant and interviewed, or had other people interview, over 700 European "rescuers" and "non-rescuers" or "bystanders" to try to discover the difference in automatic initial response, when faced with the decision of how to respond to someone who needed help.

One of the differences they discovered was in the way these people were treated as children, how they were disciplined (punishment vs. conversation to understand), and the attitudes toward "other" (people not in the family or race) of the adults in the child's life.

They learned that the rescuers were altruistic because of compassionate and un-prejudiced upbringing in the family more than anything else.

 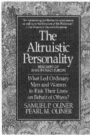 

The first book in the picture above, *Narrow Escapes*, is an autobiographical story by a local professor of his escape and life. The second one, *The Altruistic Personality*, is a joint effort by him and his wife. The third book, *Rescue, The Story of How Gentiles Saved Jews in the Holocaust*, was Michael's favorite. Through it Michael discovered the story of Oscar Schindler that is told in the movie Schlinder's List.

Conclusion

I have heard it said that adolescence is a difficult age, similar to that of the *terrible twos* that many have observed in the first stage of development, from 0-3. However we have learned over the years that when the needs of the two-year-old for concentration, independence, activity, and so on, are met, there is no such thing as a *terrible twos*, but we see instead *wonderful twos*. We found the same situation during the adolescent years.

At the end of Michael's middle school homeschooling time there was no "adolescent problem." His physical needs for sleep and lack of academic pressure had been met; the psychological need for real work had been fulfilled; the mental need to follow his interests and create his own course of study — rather than being tied to one designed by someone else — had been met. As a result, as he neared the high school years, Michael was a healthy, peaceful, constructive, joyful, funny, kind, and creative young adult.

The following quote from Montessori's book *To Educate the Human Potential*, explains very well a healthy state of mind at this time of life.

> *We shall walk together on this path of life, for all things are a part of the universe, and are connected with*

each other to form one whole unity. This idea helps the mind of the child to become fixed, to stop wandering in an aimless quest for knowledge. He is satisfied, having found the universal center of himself with all things.

NINTH GRADE

M*y vision of the future is no longer people taking exams and proceeding then on that certification . . . but of individuals passing from one stage of independence to a higher one, by means of their own activity through their own effort of will, which constitutes the inner evolution of the individual.*

— Montessori, *From Childhood to Adolescence*

This year all of Michael's friends who had completed eighth grade started their freshman year in public school. Michael decided to continue to learn at home, but after hearing them talk about school, he decided to integrate some of the elements of school he heard about.

Schedules and Goals

Michael began to self-impose schedules and goals. He kept a weekly work plan but added schedules and goals. Here is an example from his journal.

I am really working on being responsible for my work. I realized that getting into college four years from now is not a good incentive, so now if I do not finish my work on time I forfeit music for the rest of the day.

Schedule

Several of Michael's friends had to get to school an hour early for orchestra rehearsal so he experimented with sleep schedules.

From journal and work plans:

7:30 shower, dress, make bed, clean room. 7:30-8 eat
and clean up kitchen. 8:00 begin working.
I am still working on getting up on time so Jim is
waking me up now if I am still asleep.

This plan of getting up as early as his friends in high school didn't last long and we were glad. Here is up-to-date information from the National Institute of Mental Health (2020) that supports what Montessori said about adolescence:

Teens should get about 9 to 10 hours of sleep a night,
but most teens do not get enough sleep. A lack of sleep can
make it difficult to pay attention, may increase
impulsivity, and may increase the risk for irritability or
depression.

Because the teen brain is still developing, teens may
respond to stress differently than adults, which could lead
to stress-related mental disorders such as anxiety and
depression. Mindfulness, which is a psychological process
of actively paying attention to the present moment, may
help teens cope with and reduce stress.

Grades

From journal:
This week I started a grading system so I would have an
incentive to get my work done. I get a point for everything
on the list and then at the end of the week I add them up

and figure out the percentage and my grade. Last week I got a 93/100, which is a B.

I got another B this week, a 94/100, so in six weeks I should be getting 100/100, A+

Self-Imposed Deadlines

Valuable Words from a Montessori Researcher:

Although deadlines set by others have a negative effect on task interest and motivation, self-imposed deadlines do not. Indeed, studies suggest that students even work faster when they impose their own deadlines. In one study comparing self- to instructor-imposed deadlines, students who set their own deadlines for coursework complied with their self-imposed schedules better and completed work faster than students on an instructor-imposed schedules. This fits with what is known as self-determination theory: Deadlines imposed by others are demotivating because they reduce one's sense of control. When deadlines are self-administered control is maintained, so deadlines are not demotivating.

—Dr. Angeline Stoll Lillard, *Montessori, The Science Behind the Genius*, the chapter "Choice and Perceived Control"

First Band - Ring around the Sun

This year Michael and three friends formed their first band. The name was *Ring around the Sun*. In the hopes that someday they would be as famous as the Beatles they carefully recorded and labeled all of their rehearsals in case they became valuable collectors items. We remember that first rehearsal because most of the time was taken up, not by playing or discussing music, but by making plans for their album cover.

COME
AND
ENJOY!

During Tuesday Lunch,
December 23rd, 1997, 11–1

St. Vincent de Paul, Eureka, California

classic rock'n'roll music
by the new teenage band:
RING AROUND THE SUN

From Michael's journal some time later:

We had a housewarming party to celebrate moving into our own house. My band played during the party: Matt who plays rhythm guitar, Bruce on bass, Colin on drums and me on lead guitar. On the first set of three we were mostly tuning and setting up but we played Good Lovin', Bad Moon Rising, Today and the Next Day Tomorrow *(an original by me),* Heat Wave *and jamming the 12-bar blues.*

Another journal entry:

We have been invited to play at the Eureka homeless shelter on the 23rd for about two hours. We will play for about 300 to 400 people. We only have an hour of songs but we will be able to repeat. This will be our third concert.

We practiced about 20 hours and have a lot more songs including Hey Jude, Sugar Magnolia, Jack Straw, Turn on Your Lovelight.

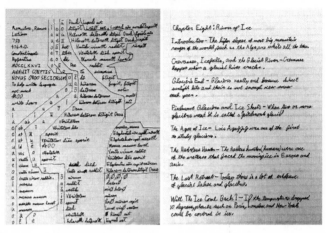

Latin

Just as in the earlier years, Michael followed his interests, researching or reading about anything that he became interested in. He continued the study of Latin through a homeschooling correspondence course. Above is a picture of his answers to one of the tests. It looks like a mind map, rather than linear answers, a way of connecting the answers in the way he thinks.

Geology

We found a geology book, *The Story of Geology*, Golden Press, that included many of the concepts from the Montessori 6-12 years, such as the creation of the earth, formation of mountains, volcanoes, earthquakes, the formation of rocks, the work of wind and currents, and so on.

I assigned a project for Michael because I wanted to follow the Montessori principle of beginning with the whole and working our way to the details, especially since he had already learned many of the details and needed an overview to put it together. This is from his journal:

> *I am learning to summarize data in a textbook. Here are the steps I take:*
>
> *1. Read all the chapter titles*
>
> *2. Read the text under the illustrations in the first chapter*
>
> *3. Summarize each of the sub headings topics in a notebook*

Michael worked for weeks on this project, ending up with many pages of summarizations of and a good understanding of geology.

Years later when Michael was in law school, a professor assigned to the students something similar, to go completely through the course text and make notes very much like what I had asked Michael to do with the geology book. He was very glad to share this with me and he saw even more the value of having done it in ninth grade.

I was giving a workshop in Hawaii to the foster parents group, and because Michael was so interested in geology and how the islands were formed one after the other over a "hot spot" between geological plates, he went with me. We flew in a helicopter looking down into the volcano on the big island of

Hawaii, followed the trail of lava peeking up here and there through the surface of the land and then over the sea where we could see the beginning of the newest, youngest, island being formed under the sea.

This resulted in even more interest in geology back at home. From his journal:

> *This week I finished six chapters outlining the geology book. Because I have been studying geology and I was visiting Narda and Ulysses in Portland, we decided to visit the Colombia River Gorge. At the end of the Ice Age when all the glaciers were melting, the Glacial Lake Missoula broke through its natural dam and flooded that part of the US. This happened 90 times.*
>
> *On our way home from Portland Jim and I went on a tour of one of the Oregon Caves. It was the largest cave I had seen. There were a lot of different insects in the cave and a lot of limestone. The cave was discovered by a man who was hunting a bear when the bear went into a cave entrance. The guide said that he was in the cave during an earthquake but they could not feel it because the cave is so stable.*

Music

Michael continued all of his music lessons and classes at the music institute. He also played in our very amateur local *Mad River Philharmonic* orchestra with Jim and me once a week. In ninth grade he took his first official for-credit music class at the university. We went with him to sign up as we were all a bit apprehensive because of his age and lack of a high school diploma, but the registrar told us that homeschoolers had a very good reputation in classes there.

After the twice a week one-hour class he sat in on many other classes in many subjects with the permission of the professors. From his journal:

> *12:00-1:00 Junior Orchestra class. 1:00-5:00 Sit in on classes, work at Michael Olaf, time off.*

Notable Concerts attended this year (thanks to our university): Marcel Marceau, Manhattan Transfer, Doc Watson, Black Umfolosi, Los Munequitos de Matanzas, Miriam Makeba, The Bulgarian Voices, Huun-Huur-Tu, Inti-Illimani, Kartik Seshadri, Pangols Ballet of Senegal

Math

From journal:

> *Today I completed the "Super Star Teachers Basic Math" video series overview for teachers.*
>
> *This included an overview of basic math functions, fractions, decimals, using a calculator, percentages, ratio and proportions, exponents and order of operations, integers, square roots, negative powers, geometry I and II, graphing in the coordinate plane, number theory, statistics, probability, measurement, problem solving techniques, solving simple equations, introduction to Algebra I.*
>
> *For a reward for finishing the series we bought a chemistry set.*

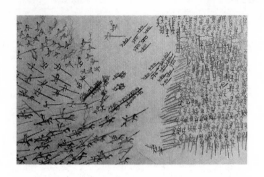

Art

Art was still part of homeschooling. Above is an intricate drawing by Michael of a battle of Samurai in ancient Japan. It was inspired by a beautiful book, *Illustrated History of Japan*, by Shigeo Nishimura. This drawing is the background of the cover of this book.

Books

Books read and recorded on weekly work plan: *Galapagos* by Kurt Vonnegut, *In My Life* by John Lennon, *Makeba My Story* by Miriam Makeba, *The Power of One* by Bryce Courtenay, *The Mahabharata, Rescue* by Milton Meltzer, *Old Peter's Russian Tales* by Arthur Ransome, *Edgar Allan Poe's Tales of Mystery and Madness, Sphere* by Michael Crichton, *Hawaii* by James Michener, *The Source* by James Michener, *Roman Record* (Usborne books), *Animal Farm* by George Orwell, *Where the Red Fern Grows* by Wilson Rawls, *Parrot in the Oven: Mi Vida* by Victor Martinez, *The Pearl* by John Steinbeck, *Hiroshima* by John Hersey, *Things Fall Apart* by Chinua Achebe, *The Complete Guitarist* by Chapman, *The Secret Life of Plants* by Peter Tompkins,

Television and Computers

As I look back on this reading record it makes me think about how valuable the book *Four Arguments for the Elimination of Television* by Jerry Mander, was for our family. We had a television that was kept in a closet and brought out for the weekly family movie, and for the Great Courses series of classes.

One week we put on the video *The Good Earth*, based on the book by Pearl S. Buck. Michael was disgusted, first because it was black and white and then because it was so slow in the beginning. He stormed back and forth between the sofa where Jim and I were seated and the TV, grumbling. Gradually he began to slow down and pay attention to what was happening in the movie. Then he sat down, leaned forward elbows on knees, watching carefully. At the end of the movie he said, "That was great. Are there any more movies like that?"

Our computer was only used for a typing tutor program, the family business work. The computer at the homeschooling school was available to individual students one hour at a time for educational games.

Research shows today how bad screen time is for infants, children, and adults so I am not going to go into that. But I will say that because we didn't watch TV or anything on computers our daily schedule was not scheduled by wanting to watch something at a particular time, and we had almost no knowledge of what we were supposed to go out and buy, and what we were supposed to look like or think, and we didn't have to worry about becoming addicted.

I would say that lack of television and computers had a lot to do with the happiness of our family over those years and the success of homeschooling.

Work Journal

Examples from Michael's weekly work plans:

soccer, work on budget, work at Michael Olaf, read in bed (most nights), shovel gravel, band practice, geology book, practice piano, practice viola, practice classical guitar, geometry [Key Curriculum Press, Berkeley California], *clean kitchen, chop firewood, plant trees, Cosmos video, save tadpoles from drying pond*

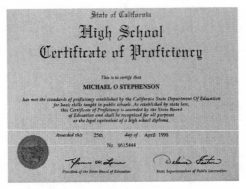

Testing out of High School

In April, near the end of the year Michael took and passed the California exam for testing out of high school. Here are the words on the certificate:

State of California High School
Certificate of Proficiency
This is to certify that Michael O. Stephenson has met the standards of proficiency established by the California

State Department of Education for the basic skills taught in public schools. As established by the state law, this Certificate of Proficiency is awarded by the State Board of Education and shall be recognized for all purposes as the legal equivalent of a high school diploma.

Now Michael would be able to take for credit some of the university classes he had been sitting in on, and he could become a certified Suzuki teacher.

TENTH GRADE

Homeschooling took place anytime, and Michael continued this year to follow his interests, and to work on creating a balance of academic work in several areas of study.

Academics

He worked on algebra and geometry in workbooks, logic on the video course, physics through simple experiments, and biology by watching and reading the "Life on Earth" and "The Living Planet" video and book series by David Attenborough. He read several books by Brian Swimme on the universe, watched French videos, studied the Socratic method of debating, *The Crito*, practiced typing tutor, and began to compose music with a computer program given to him by a musician friend in San Francisco.

Jean's School

At the end of the summer some of Michael's young friends got together with Dr. Jean Bazemore (Suzuki teacher, theatre professor, and the person who had arranged the performance at the Edinburgh Fringe Festival). They asked her if it would be possible to create a high school that was more like Suzuki Summer Academy — the work collaborative rather than competitive, older children able to care for and work with the younger ones, learning enjoyable and creative, respect for oneself, each other, and the environment.

Never one to turn down a new educational possibility she said, "Yes." Thus began a small alternative high school named "Jean's School."

For the first semester Michael and several students met at Jean's house three mornings a week. In the words of Tyler, the friend with whom Michael had gone to Peru:

> *We read books.* Pride and Prejudice, Moby Dick, The Iliad *and* The Odyssey, *etc. We wrote papers and reflections. We played music. We listened to the ocean and the birds. We wrote and performed skits about our history lessons.*

Colin Stevens, a British humanitarian, activist, and actor who often taught at the Suzuki Summer Academy in Trinidad, California came from England to work and teach with Jean. In the second semester Jean's School expanded to five mornings a week. Most of the students had arranged an independent study through Arcata High School to be able to attend Jean's School part-time. Subjects that were not taught at Jean's school they took at the local high school.

Math: Michael and Jim took an algebra class together at the university (graphing calculators, graphing equations).

Theatre: Michael registered for a university theatre class along with the other students. This was a class given by Jean during which they studied theatre and performed two plays.

History: The history assignments at Jean's School were from Howard Zinn's book *A People's History of the United States* (1980 version). The students had assignments and discussions each week based on this book, and on The New York Times and other articles that brought history up to the present. For example Greece in the past and Greece in the present, and the situation in Kosovo related to its history and that of Eastern Europe.

From Michael's journal:

> *History is the study of things that, even if we would like them to, can never be changed. It is feeling the emotions of people who lived hundreds or even thousands of years ago. It is playing the music of composers who lived before our time in places all over the world, reading the poetry of past wordsmiths, playing the sports of children from many centuries, acting the parts of works by playwrights such as Shakespeare and Moliere, and criticizing, praising, and contemplating the thoughts and ides of philosophers like Socrates and Plato. When our understanding of history progresses, we start seeing why our world is the way it is.*

Michael's history research and papers included *Herodotus and History*, and *A vindication of Women's Rights* by Mary Wollstonecraft,

French: Three of the students including Michael continued to study French with weekly tests.

English: Years later Michael still has detailed and enjoyable memories of the significance of each of the Montessori grammar symbols, and his homeschool independent study of Latin reinforces his understanding of grammar. But Jean and Colin really helped Michael improve his writing.

The text for English was *The Conscious Reader*, by Caroline Shrodes. This book, updated regularly, represents a broad range of interests such as art, cultural studies, education, psychology, philosophy, politics, science, technology and environmental studies. *Sound and Sense, an Introduction to Poetry*, by Laurence Perrine was also used as a test.

For research papers, the student had to explain his or her choice. Then provide a lot of documented research and several drafts of each paper over the semester, along with detailed references, and give a well-rehearsed dramatic presentation (not just reading).

Michael's papers included:

My Opinion on the Cause of Iphigenia's Death (Greek Mythology).

Dante's *The Divine Comedy*. The final presentation of *The Divine Comedy* to the group included printed illustrations from the artist Gustave Doré.

This is from his journal on a paper about Claude Debussy:

The Life and Music of Claude Debussy

A couple of months ago I saw the movie Round Midnight. *It is a movie about some jazz musicians living in Paris. In the movie some of the musicians regarded Claude Debussy as the founder of jazz theory. Since I was interested in jazz I started reading about Debussy and his*

*music. Soon afterwards Charles Fulkerson, who had been
teaching me some jazz piano, said that I should study
music by Debussy and he loaned me some books on this
musician. Also I have heard references to Debussy in post-
Debussy music; for example his use of whole tone scales is
mirrored in a lot of free jazz. A more particular example
would be the comparison of the chord changes in his*
Danseuses de Delphes *and the Grateful Dead's* Doin'
that Rag.

His presentation of the Debussy paper included playing examples on the piano of the points he was making about the connection between Debussy's music and jazz. Jean asked him to record it to be presented over the university radio station.

Jean had only taught at the university level and she expected the same quality of work from these high school freshmen and sophomores, but they didn't disappoint her.

University Credit: At Humboldt State University Michael earned six credits this year, five credits for the fall semester for the algebra class (Graphing Calculator), theater (Historical Perspective in Theatre, Modern Drama), and Percussion Ensemble. For the spring semester he earned another credit for music (Percussion Ensemble-Calypso Band).

Music

Idyllwild: In July, Jim and Michael and I attended the Idyllwild Arts summer camp in Southern California. Michael studied jazz full time for a week, with faculty concerts in the evenings, and Jim and I took art classes, taught 60's music on

238

guitar to the students, answered questions about our anti-war political years, and led the young people on a procession through the camp singing "We Shall Overcome." Michael's counselor was Ari Shapiro who you can now hear on the news on NPR (The Public Broadcasting Company).

Suzuki Teacher Training: Having a high school diploma enabled Michael to study to become a certified Suzuki piano teacher, registered with a Suzuki Association of the Americas diploma. In August he and his two friends, Andrea and Collin, were driven by Andrea's father to the Conservatory at Mount Royal College in Calgary, Alberta, Canada to begin the teacher training courses for *Suzuki Foundations*, and *Suzuki Piano Book One*. They camped on the way, mostly listened to 60's music (Collin's idea), and lived partly on cheese pizza (Michael's preference).

Here are some of Michael's notes from the Suzuki teacher-training course. I think they sound very much like Montessori teaching:

> *Learning begins at birth, learn through senses, small steps, train ear first as tone develops technique, ability develops ability, look for good things and build on them, child sets the time frame for learning, be flexible, celebrate the process not just the product, be patient, love the child.*

Suzuki Summer Academy: Having been one of the students at camp since it opened, now Michael was a teacher. During the summer of 1997 Michael had taught guitar at the Suzuki

Summer Academy and this year he had students in guitar, piano, and xylophone.

First Music Tour

In December the HSU Percussion Ensemble, one of Michael's music ensembles, gave a public performance at the university and the following semester they went on a week tour to Oregon and Washington. The famous musician from Trinidad and Tobago, Ray Holman, performed with them.

Second Music/Drama Tour

The highlight of this second semester at Jean's School was a performance trip to Europe. Michael had always earned much of the cost of his trips working at our family business, but now he was also giving private piano lessons to children and adults, and so he was able to earn more.

The group of students called themselves *The Young Actors' Guild*. In Florence, Italy and Paris, France they performed the two plays they had learned and performed at the university at home. These were *Trifles* by Susan Glaspell, and *Aria da Capo* by Edna St. Vincent Millay both plays addressing gender issues in the USA at the turn of the century.

In the play *Trifles* Michael wore a suit and played a district attorney. Everyone said he made a very good lawyer and that is what he has become.

Paris meant a lot to Michael because of his interest in Debussy, Erik Satie, Manet, and Degas.

From his journal:

> As I sit at the piano in the International High School in Paris, playing my own musical ideas on a jazz piece "Black Orpheus" for the students of the school, and thinking about the American plays we are presenting to children on this trip, I feel so lucky to be part of the tradition of learning and sharing the arts through travel and exposure of many other people in the world.

They saw a play at the Comedie-Francaise, which was completely in French but made the point that there is a lot more than just spoken language to make a drama successful. They visited the Rodin Museum, and saw Paris from the top of the Eiffel Tower.

In Florence they performed in the streets. This was something Michael's father, Jim, had done in Amsterdam and Paris years earlier, after graduating from Commedia dell'arte, so Michael had heard the stories and was familiar with the tradition of street performances.

From his journal:

It is windy, blowing lots of viewers towards our stage. Our music starts and hundreds of children are caught by it. As we begin the actions and the lines, a crowd gathers to watch and as each spectator moves on another one takes its place and so there is a myriad of eyes watching at all times. Under this pressure we realize that it is a reasonable thing to ask that we do our best.

Another journal entry:

It was nine o'clock, dark outside, a safe and beautiful place to explore and to learn. The sound of instruments drew us out into the night's street, musicians playing saxophones, drums, guitars, and violins.

These musicians inspired us to find a place to play music. Finally we came to a quiet side street with little traffic, which we decided was a good place. Collin and Bruce started to play the African Djembe drums that they had bought here in Florence. Soon I joined. A man named Rolando approached us. How did we know his name? He did not speak English and we did not speak Italian. Point to self "Me, Michael" "Me, Rolando". Age old communication.

Rolando started teaching us how to get different sounds from his own Djembe. Then he gave us another lesson; with hand gestures, he instructed Collin to take off his shoes. He then gestured for us to continue playing the drums as he proceeded to hold up the shoe in request for money from the pedestrians passing by. We could tell from

*their expressions that these people were surprised at the
sight of several young Americans in the company of a
middle-aged Italian man asking for lire. But we soon
realized that people seemed to think this was normal
behavior. They smiled and threw coins into the shoe.*

*This experience more than any other showed us that
through music we could start communicating and
participating in the happiness of people despite barriers of
experience, language, and cultural differences.*

Continuing to Homeschool

Michael learned a lot about writing, performing, and
history and literature through this experience at Jean's School,
and he enjoyed studying with good friends. But at the end of
the year he decided that the required homework was
preventing him from having time for his other interests,
including music. So he decided to return to homeschooling for
eleventh grade, his junior high school year.

He still found time to read, including at night before
going to sleep. His personal reading list for the year contained:
Stranger in a Strange Land by Robert Heinlein, *Slaughterhouse-
Five* by Kurt Vonnegut, *There are No Children Here, The Story of
Two Boys Growing Up in The Other America* by Alex Kotlowitz,
Sherlock Holmes: The Seven Percent Solution by David Tipton
and others, *Freckles* by Gene Stratton Porter, *Into the Wild* by
Jon Krakauer, *Coverup* by Jay Bennett, *A State of Blood* by Hen
Kyemba (about Idi Amin in Uganda), and *The Einstein Paradox,
And Other Science Mysteries Solved by Sherlock Holmes* by Colin
Bruce

PSAT (preliminary scholastic aptitude test)

This year, in October Michael's average PSAT score for verbal, math, and writing was 61%. In June his score for verbal was 81% and math 65%. Without much in the way of traditionally required subjects, Michael was keeping up. We thought that score was fine for a person who had, except for in Jean's School during tenth grade, not taken the classes, from first grade through tenth grade, on which these standardized tests are based.

We didn't see the value of spending years following a curriculum decided by others. It continued to be more important to us that Michael be able to follow an independent path, to enjoy — and thus remember — what he learned, to be a good teacher for the young, and most of all to continue to search for a way to contribute to the solutions of the future from a broad and unique perspective.

> *Joy, feeling one's own value, being appreciated and loved by others, feeling useful and capable of production are all factors of enormous value for the human soul.*
> — Montessori, *From Childhood to Adolescence*

Service

Michael and some fellow music students often played music at the Alzheimer's Center. Here is something he wrote about one of those experiences:

> *A former piano teacher, after each piece, would speak enthusiastically about how great the songs were and about what a great time she was having. And for us, the*

performers? I think I speak for each one of us when I say
that it is wonderful to be given a chance to perform
something that we have been working hard at and at the
same time to be giving a very special gift to some people
who really need it.

But he did not have a regular, repeated, way of being of service and he was looking for a way. Our family had become close friends with Charles Fulkerson, well-loved university piano professor and director of the Humboldt Symphony Orchestra for many years, because we were in the local Mad River philharmonic together. Charles had become too old to drive so we started picking him up before the rehearsal, even though he lived just a few blocks away, and then would visit with him after. We also took him for drives on the weekend and often to concerts, always followed by his insistence that we stop on the way home for ice cream no matter how late it was.

One day we asked Charles if he would like Michael to fix him lunch once a week and he was thrilled. So on Michael's weekly work plan he always put "fix lunch for Charles" on Friday morning, sometimes recording the kind of soup he was going to make.

Charles had stopped teaching piano years earlier but after a few weeks of soup he started asking Michael to play for him and then started teaching him. One day he asked Michael to tell him what he would like to learn and Michael said "Great Balls of Fire" by Jerry Lewis. That was not part of Charles repertoire but he started helping Michael learn more modern music and then jazz improvisation. Mostly they had a lot of fun together.

Losing a Friend

On a Thursday in March 1999 Charles asked his daughter Julie to phone us to say that he would not need soup the next day. The next day Charles died while taking a nap. Julie phoned us and Michael and I drove down to say goodbye. Michael played the piano just in case Charles could hear him, all of the music that the two of them had worked on and enjoyed together.

ELEVENTH GRADE

W̶e no longer thought of Michael as anything but an adult. He was in charge of his life, his schedule, and his education. Of course we were there for him whenever he needed us just as we were for any family member, but he was very independent and responsible. For the most part no one had told him what he should study, what he should think, who he should be. He was healthy, happy, and busy being creative and learning and teaching.

Building a Music Studio

Near the end of tenth grade, overhearing Michael say to a friend one day that it would be wonderful to have his own studio for band practice and teaching, Jim and I suggested he research the possibility. He made a list of his potential earnings and contacted John and Alice, the couple who had been the contractors for our home and were now good friends.

This is from his journal:

> *May 3 - Susan and I drew plans of an 18' x 24"*
> *music studio. John and Alice came over for dinner and we*
> *looked over the plans. John suggested a perimeter*
> *foundation, plywood exterior. I figured out that if Jim paid*
> *for the foundation, and if we used B grade, used, doors, I*
> *could earn the money for the rest.*
>
> *May 10 - John gave us an estimate. We decided not*
> *to have water and to have a composting toilet so no*
> *plumbing. Today we worked on the floor plan to decide*
> *where to put piano, windows, door, etc.*

May 19 – The Backhoe came and dug trenches for the foundation.

Michael was still keeping the kind of careful budget he had begun years ago but now all of the earnings went toward the cost of the studio. Jim had never built anything or done much in the way of working with wood but he was interested in learning.

Together Jim and Michael went to the library and checked out books and videos on construction. John and Alice came over periodically to check on progress. One day, when Michael and several friends whom he had called for help had pulled the wall framing into place, the framing began to buckle. John came over and helped the group secure everything with rope so they could get roof beams in place to hold everything together.

Another time when my father, an engineer, was visiting and we were trying to figure out how to get the large sheets of plywood lifted on to the roof beams, my father was thrilled to be able to guide us. Another time Michael and our visiting future son-in-law Chip, donned facemasks and insulated the studio. Many people were glad to help with this project.

When it was time to tile the roof Michael, who does not like to be up high, hired two local fishermen who had a little experience in this area and needed work. It was certainly a family-community project and there was plenty for Michael to learn in the process.

You can read more about this project in the twelfth grade, the next chapter, because Michael wrote about it in his college applications.

Teaching Music

Summer: During the summer Michael attended the next level of the Suzuki teacher-training program, this time at Holy Names College in Oakland, California. It covered Suzuki Piano Book Two, and analyzed the music of books Seven and Eight. The training included observations of lessons given by master teachers, and being observed while giving lessons.

During the Year: Michael was now on the teaching staff at the HSU Music Academy at Humboldt State University, teaching piano and guitar. Here is his bio on the Faculty Biographies description page: *(jazz piano, jazz guitar, percussion) Suzuki certification Calgary Conservatory and Holy Names College; Stanford University Jazz Workshop; Idyllwild Jazz; HSU student; local private teacher*

By the end of the eleventh grade school year Michael was teaching adults and children in his music studio.

From his Journal: *I have moved all of my stuff to the studio and am teaching there.*

Playing Music

Here is a list of music groups Michael was in in eleventh grade:

Sequoia Chamber Music Workshop – plays viola

HSU Marimba band – plays marimba

HSU Percussion Ensemble – plays steel drum

HSU Symphonic Band – plays piano

HSU Symphony Orchestra – playing percussion

HSU PM Jazz Band – plays piano

HSU The Yellow Combo – plays piano

HSU Calypso Band – plays double tenor steel drum

From the newspaper: *The Humboldt Calypso Band, which has performed with some of the best steel bands in the world, prides itself in maintaining an accurate, authentic connection to the roots of the steel band movement and the innovative musicians of Trinidad* (the Caribbean island), *where this unique percussion phenomenon was born.*

From Michael's journal:

I went to see the "Wicked Cooks" play because the person who is doing the music and sound effects is not able to do it the next night so I am going to fill in. I watched what he was doing and how it cued in with the actor's lines. The next night Jim, Susan, Karin and Ursula came to watch. I played marimba for the most part, some military stuff on the snare drum and some other

percussion instruments for sound effects. I had fun and I
learned a lot. It was a good experience to get it together so
quickly with little rehearsal

There were many, many journal and work-schedule entries about giving music lessons, music practice, music performances attended, and music rehearsals with friends (what they played, who played what instruments, the key signatures, and more).

Academics

In Michael's junior year he again took classes at HSU (Humboldt State University). He would take the bus back and forth from Trinidad to Arcata. He earned six credits in the fall taking *Jazz-An American Art Form*, and two performance classes, *Chamber Ensemble - Percussion*, and *Calypso Band.*

In the Spring semester he earned thirteen credits: *Contemporary Math-Statistics* (a practical class as it applied to what Michael was learning in our family business, and in his interest in politics), *Physics-Descriptive Astronomy* (the professor, Dr. Steve Brusca was so good and so famous that one had to be on the waiting list to get into his classes), and performance classes including *Jazz Big Band, Chamber Ensemble Jazz, Chamber Ensemble Percussion, Humboldt Symphony Orchestra.*

Since Michael has not had the usual pre-requisite classes for these math and science classes he didn't do so well in these classes in the beginning.

From his journal:

I need to spend more time on astronomy and math. I did really badly on my statistics midterm on Monday.

So he asked a friend who he knew from his Mistwood homeschooling years to tutor him in math and physics. Marc was a research engineer at the Schatz Energy Research Center at the university. Here is some of what Marc wrote about Michael later as part of a college recommendation:

Michael has always been mature for his age and unusually self-possessed. It would be hard not to be impressed with Michael's outstanding musical accomplishments and all that they indicate about his self-discipline, diligence, maturity, and dedication; indeed everyone but Michael is. His demeanor is quiet, modest and respectful to all those with whom he comes into contact. He is exceptionally cultured, a gentleman, well liked by peers and adults. I was very impressed with how sharp he is, how quickly he grasped mathematical and scientific concepts, and the enthusiasm and perceptiveness he brought to our sessions, which included wide-ranging discussions of applied math, computer science, and astrophysics.

Michael earned a grade of B in astronomy. Statistics was a credit/no credit class and he earned a C+. He earned A's on all of the music classes.

Work at Home

Michael continued to follow interests. Here are some notes from his junior year journal and weekly schedule:

> I read a play called Tartuffe by Moliere. The Chinn family and their exchange student from Thailand came over. Wesley and Alison sang while Daryl played piano songs from Don Giovanni and Les Miserables. Today started with feeding the animals as usual. Colin and I played "007 Goldeneye" on his new Nintendo. On New Years' Eve we went to three parties and sang Auld Lang Syne at each one. Finished reading The Martian Chronicles. Math homework. Astronomy homework.
>
> (May 21) I am spending all my time studying for the ACT and the SAT and trying to figure out my life.
>
> (June) Tomorrow morning I take the SAT. I have learned a lot in the last few weeks and it will not only be helpful for the test but also for the rest of my education.

Correspondence courses: Michael took two courses from the Great Courses video library (thegreatcourses.com) that is often used by homeschoolers. Highly rated high school and college teachers give the lectures and there are also workbooks or "guidebooks". The best thing is that one can move at one's own pace, covering several chapters in one day or perhaps doing one chapter and then mental processing it for several weeks before continuing.

(1) *How to Become a SuperStar Student*: Included topics of this course are: recognizing one's learning style, taking

effective notes, learning to schedule and prioritize work, solving problems with creativity and critical thinking, and approaching tests with focus.

(2) *An Introduction to Formal Logic*: From the course introduction: *Flawed, misleading, and false arguments are everywhere. From advertisers trying to separate you from your money, to politicians trying to sway your vote, to friends who want you to agree with them.*

Michael has often said that, unlike some math (the daily required worksheet type), which he forgot and considered a waste of precious time, he remembered everything he had learned studying logic. Jim and I had both studied logic at university and were so very glad to share this appreciation of the subject and logical thinking with Michael.

Thinking About Going Away to School

Michael was content to stay in California and concentrate on music and classes at HSU, but Dr. Eugene Novotney, one of his mentors and fellow musicians told us that Michael should move out and challenge himself against other scholars and musicians. Michael respected this person and agreed to think about it.

At this time Stanford University had a section of their website for homeschooler applications. We contacted them and were told that we should create a list of Michael's education so far and bring it to Stanford, which we did. A counselor there helped us put it into a format that was accepted everywhere Michael applied. He was not able to apply to the University of California system because they required the standard traditional high school classes in math and sciences. But there were many other choices.

During a trip for a Montessori conference on the East Coast, where our company exhibited materials, we visited several universities. There just happened to be a lecture by an admissions counselor at Harvard University while we were there so we attended. There were hundreds of people in the audience and when taking questions the speaker would ask what high school the person was attending; he seemed to know a lot about high schools all over the country. He told us that Harvard receives hundreds of applicants from students who had taken all of the right classes, had top grades, were valedictorians, and earned perfect college entrance exam scores, but admissions are looking for something more. I don't remember his exact words in describing "more" but they aligned with what we were doing—real experience of creative thinking, responsibility, initiative, independence, and helping others as a lifestyle and not as just something to look good on a college application.

Michael wanted to be sure that he would be able to pursue music in an excellent music department no matter what so that was our focus. He searched for schools that had a steel drum ensemble and Brown University met his requirements so we were sure to visit Brown.

TWELFTH GRADE

It was a joy to live daily life with this thoughtful, hardworking, creative person, and to never know what he was going to do next. We saw his passion for music as one of many possible paths to pursue. As parents we had followed many different paths, as had his sisters, and we anticipated that Michael would do the same.

Teaching Music

Michael's private lessons, teaching children and adults, were now held either in his new studio or in the music building at Humboldt State University.

Again this year he was on the faculty of the Humboldt Music Academy at the university, teaching piano, guitar, and percussion

Michael now was the teacher of a jazz combo for Jean's School, and they practiced in his music studio. This was a wonderful musical experience as old friends from early childhood formed the group.

> *Andrea on piano, Bruce guitar, Conner Sax, Riley Bass, Collin joining the school group to play drums and percussion, and me on drums.*

Playing Music

The summer before twelfth grade Michael again attended the Sequoia Chamber Music workshop for two weeks held at the university.

For the most part Michael was in the same groups or ensembles as in eleventh grade, practicing regularly and participating in performances. He also often was part of new groups forming. And sometimes he had the experience of touring with a music group. For example, his HSU Percussion Ensemble performed at the 16th annual Northwest Percussion Festival at the University of Oregon School of Music.

Kachimbo

Michael had recently become part of the Afro-Cuban band Kachimbo, better described in this newspaper article:

> *Kachimbo, the most authentic and superb representation of Afro-Cuban Music, has been together since 1994, and have produced several CDs one of which was nominated for a Grammy award. Several members of the band have been to Cuba and although they appreciate the different styles of Cuban music they play contemporary forms and are one of the few salsa bands that play* timba, *the latest salsa from Cuba. Its newest members are Dr. Eugene Novotney, HSU instructor and internationally recognized performer and composer of classical music, and Michael Stephenson, a "musical*

prodigy and a great soloist, exciting and very playful",
according to David Peñalosa, head of the band.

Academics

In the fall of Michael's senior year he took a second physics class from Dr. Brusca, called *The Cosmos*. On his weekly schedule, study for that class was listed for every weekday. I think that the preparation based on the first Montessori great lesson, the creation of the solar system and the earth, might have had something to do with his interest in this class.

Although Michael continued to take classes from the videos offered by TheGreatCourses.com (such as literature and business) the cosmology class at the university was the last official academic class of Michael's high school years. At the end of twelfth grade he had earned thirty-one credit hours from Humboldt State University with a grade point average of B+.

However, knowing that he would now be required to catch up on the work his peers had been doing in traditional schools, he took on the task of preparing for college entrance exams as part of his at-home academic work for the year. He worked from practice tests in books, with a computer program, and also by taking practice ACT and SAT tests.

Work at Home

From his journal: *clean room, clean kitchen, read Cosmos* [from the HSU class], *feed cats, restock both firewood piles, watch business video* [another course

258

from GreatCourses.com], *Spanish, math* [probably from the SAT/ACT preparation], *compare notes from business class video course with Jim* [our family business as the real-life information], *note-taking practice* [from the SuperStar Student video course], *clean studio, wash the outside of both cars, piano lesson with Yumi* [learning from her, not teaching her], *Literature* Video (world literature course from The Great Courses), *piano performance seminar*

Instead of our usual family Holiday newsletter this year Michael created a CD of music to share with grandparents, friends, and other family members. It included: "Camaguey" performed by Kachimbo, "Guachi Guara" performed by The HSU Calypso Band, "Connected Forces" performed by the HSU Percussion Ensemble, and two classical piano pieces performed by Michael at the Sequoia Chamber Music Workshop at HSU.

Applying to University

For the second time, because of a Montessori conference where our Jim and Michael and I would be exhibiting educational materials, we visited schools on the East Coast.

Although he was not sure that he wanted to leave for university we explained to him that although it would be his choice, if he wanted to be accepted and to receive a need-based scholarship, which would be necessary for him to attend a private university, he had to apply during his senior high school year.

Then he could take a gap year between high school and university. He agreed, which is why he was spending time in preparation for the SAT and ACT exams.

By fall Michael had decided to apply early admissions to Brown University. When we had visited he was disappointed to find that there was no longer a steel drum ensemble, which was one of the reasons he was interested in this university. But he had learned a lot about Brown since then that he really liked. For example, there is no prescribed curriculum at Brown, even for freshman. Students are recommended to explore very widely but it is their choice. Also, one has the choice to take each course for pass/fail or for a grade.

This seemed very much like Michael's homeschooling years, free choice of studies, following interested without thinking about competition, and no temptation to take a class just because it was easy to get a good grade.

Michael was accepted by early admission at Brown so he did not pursue applications for other schools.

College Essays

We thought it would be interesting to include Michael's Brown University application essays, one part was required to be handwritten, and the other typed. They briefly sum up his own perspective on his homeschooling experience.

The Handwritten Essay:

> *One aspect of my life that is unique is the fact that I did not go to elementary or high school. I had already gone to a Montessori preschool before I decided that I wanted to*

start homeschooling, so I had an idea about what kind of education worked for me. I like to choose one or two subjects at a time, and to immerse myself into those areas. At one point I became very interested in the history of ancient Rome. I read many books on the Romans, studied the architecture, arches, roads, and waterways, and I rented the "I Claudius" series of videos, and read the books. I even went with my parents to Rome where I got to see the Roman Coliseum and other famous sites of Roman history. Some of the pictures I drew in Rome ended up on the cover of an educational catalogue.

I have had many unique experiences as a result of my alternative education. One that comes readily to mind is the building of my music studio. I had quite a few music students that I had been teaching in our living room. This was always very disruptive for my mother because she works in her office at home. Also the studio would become my private composing and practicing space. There was a lot of work involved in building the studio, planning things like size, shape, location and a million other details. I had to plan where all the instruments and furniture were going to go. I had to budget money very carefully and save my earnings as a music teacher to pay for building supplies. There was a lot of hard manual labor involved. It was a great experience because I learned to appreciate the work of builders. I learned a lot about construction and architecture, planning of time and money, and even about eating well to keep my energy up. Most of all I learned the value of hard work. My dad and I finished the studio in a little over one year.

It is great educational experiences like these that have made me thankful for my homeschool education. I have not had to divide my day into one-hour segments for each subject. No one has set limits on how much I can devote myself and my time to a particular interest. I have been permitted to create art and music, to read, and to have time to be by myself and think. Most importantly, I have learned to enjoy working hard and learning.

The Typed Essay:

Last spring I met with Shep Shapiro of the music department who convinced me to apply to liberal arts colleges instead of conservatories because I am interested not only in music, but also in music related to many other fields. I would like to know more about how music affects human emotions and intelligence, the physics of sound, and the role of music in different cultures and time periods.

Ethnomusicology is a combination of my two main interests, music and anthropology. I have studied and played samba (Brazil), salsa (Cuba, Puerto Rico), calypso (Trinidad and Tobago, West Africa), reggae (Jamaica) European classical music and music from Iraq, India, and others. When I compose I like to incorporate elements from different styles, for example the theory from Indian Ragas with the rhythms of Cuban rhumba played on European classical instruments. I am a member of a professional Cuban salsa band and have played music with people in other countries. It is great to be able to communicate without speaking the same language.

Because I am home schooled, I am able to find the best teachers, take the most interesting classes and immerse myself in the area I am most fascinated with at the moment. Brown's respect for students' decisions about what to study is what attracted me to the school. I was a little worried that students might just take the easiest classes and not be serious about learning. But when I visited and talked to friends from home and other students they were excited about their classes and working hard. My dream has been to be in a place where everyone is studying what they choose.

I become a better student by being a teacher and a better teacher by being a student. Every week I give eight private music lessons in classical piano, jazz piano, violin, guitar, or percussion. And every week I play in several music ensembles, take class at the university, and study other subjects at home.

When I was fourteen, the director of the Suzuki Summer Academy in Trinidad, California, which I had been attending for several years, asked if I would teach some of her piano students. The following summer she arranged to have me go the Calgary Conservatory in Canada to become a certified Suzuki piano teacher. The first time I taught at the Suzuki Summer Academy I was very nervous. I was worried that the students would not treat me like a teacher because I was so young. We began the lesson by bowing to each other, which is traditional in Suzuki teaching. These students have had Suzuki music lessons before so this was a reassuring beginning for all of us. As the lesson progressed we started to have fun. I helped them with the songs that they had been working on and we played some musical games. The lesson ended with us all laughing and looking forward to the next lesson.

One of the problems that I have had with teaching is tuition. When I teach at the summer camp or at the music academy in town, the directors send me a check at the end of each term. But with the students that I teach privately at my house, I often have trouble keeping track of how much money they owe me or if they already have paid me. It is one of the most awkward situations I have ever been in to have to ask one of my student's parents for money, but I have had to ask a couple of times.

I have found that teaching is completely different from anything I have ever done before. Both the child and the parent(s) are looking up to me as well as looking to me for role models. Music teaching has improved my people skills because it is very important for the success of a lesson that everyone involved is comfortable and wants to be at the lesson. I have become very good at helping the parent and child feel at home and relaxed at the lesson. I enjoy giving music lessons because not only is it very fulfilling to see my students improve over time, but it also improves my own music. There is nothing like teaching to improve one's own grasp of the basics. It is a chance to go back and work with all the areas that I might have missed in my own musical study.

Teaching has greatly improved my education and my personality. I can really appreciate the effort any teacher is

putting into the subject, whether it is a music class or an
astronomy lecture. My teaching is not just preparation for
my later life and it is not just a hobby. It is work that is
both valid and valued.

University Recommendations

Because Michael had more students than teachers at this time he asked his music students and their parents to write his college recommendations.

Cuba

In the spring, Michael's last international trip during his homeschooling years took him, his sister Ursula, and the Kachimbo drummer, to Cuba. This was a combination of learning about other cultures and how to go about daily life in another country, and to improve musical awareness and abilities. The reason for the trip was to film Cuban dancers and musicians for making a promotional music video for an upcoming CD release.

Michael, Ursula, and Rama flew from San Francisco to Havana through Cancun, Mexico. Visas were not necessary because travel restrictions to Cuba only applied to flights originating in the USA. Rama had already been to Cuba several times. They stayed in the bedroom of a friend of Rama's, and for 2.5 weeks frugally shopped, mostly for beans and rice and juice, cooked, and cleaned, as though they lived there.

As with many kinds of musical traditions it is considered part of learning music as a musician to be able to dance it first. They took both salsa dance and music lessons. Ursula had been studying dance for years, lately African and salsa dance. Rama was also good at Latin dance and Michael worked hard to catch up with them. He tells us about one moment of the trip where he was standing on the base of a sculpture high above hundreds of people listening to a large group of street musicians. Every single person, from infants to the aged, was moving in unison in time with the rhythms of the music.

The three of them saw twenty great bands, audiotaped about 24 hours of music, and video taped more. They had 10-15 hours of Batá (a type of Cuban drum) and salsa lessons. They got the cost of meals down to about fifty cents each and spent their money (cash carried in money belts) on music, for example buying paper for Michael to record the charts of the music they were hearing or variations he was beginning to compose for the band back home.

Michael later said the most frustrating thing about the trip was having all of this musical inspiration with no instruments at hand.

Music Plus

As you have seen throughout this book, music was only one of many passions and interests that Michael explored during the homeschooling years. Our family, including Michael's sisters, are interested in many things: Narda works in the medical field, Ursula's passion was river rafting and saving the rivers. We all shared our interests with each other, but in the end allowed Michael to forge his own path, while we got out of the way.

In college Michael traveled to the favelas in Brazil, Robben Island in South Africa, the Serengeti in Tanzania East Africa, and several countries in Asia. After graduating from Brown University he volunteered for The Energy and Resources Institute in New Delhi, India and attended The Delhi Sustainable Development Summit in 2005. He later received a law degree from the University of Oregon School of Law.

Today Michael is a musician, and the head of his own law firm that also helps educate the public about bicycle law and safety. He supports environmental and humanitarian causes, rescues abandoned dogs and cats, and has many good friends. He balances his life with law work, academic and intellectual pursuits, and music; he shares the household chores, and many interests, with his wife who is a ballet dancer and a lawyer running the law firm with Michael.

If you want to learn more about Michael's music you can search for his bands *Timbata*, *Karmanauts*, and *Michel Olaf* on YouTube.

FINAL THOUGHTS

The Purpose of Education

Schools have, for many years, been thought of as institutions to prepare human beings to succeed in the future, a future that at one time was relatively stable and predictable. The future is no longer either.

Schools were thought of as places to prepare humans for specific professions that were valuable in society. The kinds of professions that will be needed in the future today are unknown. New skills and professions are coming to the fore every day, and others are becoming obsolete.

Young people today are aware of the problems that face the whole world, yet they are being asked to study subjects that do not seem to have anything to do with preparing them to have a valuable role in the future. Learning to obey, memorize, study exactly the same subjects as everyone else, fill after-school time with homework, more classes, and entertainment, allows no time for contemplation and can make young people feel helpless and hopeless.

I have found this situation to be true wherever modern college-prep academics have become the main focus of education, even in such varied places as Sikkim and Switzerland. There is too much academic pressure, and not enough understanding of children and young adults.

Study need not be restricted by the curricula of
exiting secondary [age 12-18] *schools and still less need*
we make use of their methods of dealing with the children

or instilling culture. We must say at once that the aim
should be to widen education instead of restricting it.
—Montessori, *From Childhood to Adolescence*

Montessori

The word *Montessori* is often misused in describing materials and schools, so learning as much as possible about what Montessori is — an aid to life — is essential. The website: www. montessori . edu is a good starting place.

If schools are going to truly prepare human beings to face the unpredictable with courage, wisdom, and farsightedness, following some of the principles presented in this book can be helpful. The focus then will not be just on Montessori materials and lessons, but on gaining knowledge about human development, helping children to gain physical and mental independence, to be adaptable, and to be able to analyze new situations and solve new problems. We must prepare them to question life and traditions, and to experience first-hand how it feels to be a balanced, contributing, appreciated member of a family and community.

There are Montessori programs today for helping the elderly, infants, gifted children and those with special needs; there is research on how to use Montessori ideas in sports. In none of these educational areas is a recipe provided. Our homeschooling story was the same, finding a way to use Montessori principles.

Times have changed, and science has made great
progress, and so has our work; but our principles have
only been confirmed, and along with them our conviction

that [humankind] *can hope for a solution to its problems,*
among which the most urgent are those of peace and
unity, only by turning its attention and energies to the
discovery of the child and to the development of the great
potentialities of the human personality in the course of its
formation.

—Montessori, *The Discovery of the Child*

Family and Community

Being a valuable member of a community begins with the family, at birth. From the beginning of life it is important for children to learn that every member of a community, at first the family, is equally important, equally valuable. Every human being, at any age, wants to be part of a community where their being and skills are accepted and appreciated, where they do not have to become someone else in order to be loved. When this group is the family or the classroom young people will not have to look elsewhere.

Time

When the purpose of education, Montessori, and the value of the family and community are understood there is still the question of *time*.

The strengthening of our family bonds, and Michael spending time with the very old and very young in our community, was a vital element of our homeschooling. But along with the time to learn and teach and enjoy each other, there was time to contemplate. Time, so precious today as we rush from one thing to the next, was valued and planned for in all of our lives over the years.

Even though Michael had a weekly plan of academic and other work to complete, there was plenty of time for thinking. He was free to stop working, to sit quietly and process, to take a nap, to go for a walk outside; in other words he was free to NOT work in the usual sense of the word. As a result he learned to create a healthy balance — mental and physical work, practicing music, teaching, taking classes, spending time with family and friends, physical exercise of many kinds, thinking, resting, reading. This freedom was vital to his creativity and it was practical preparation for life.

> *From an article entitled "A Better Way to Work",*
> *that explores the work habits of Darwin, Dickens, Ingmar*
> *Bergman, and others:*
>
> *They only spent a few hours a day doing what we*
> *would recognize as their most important work. The rest of*
> *the time they were hiking mountains, taking naps, going*
> *on walks with friends, or just sitting and thinking. Maybe*
> *the key to unlocking the secret of their creativity lies in*
> *understanding not just how they labored but how they*
> *rested.*

—Susan Stephenson, *Montessori and Mindfulness*

Our Family Today

We are a close, respectful, laughing and loving family and that is a precious result of our homeschooling years. Michael has benefited immensely from his education and so have Jim and I. Jim uses a lot of what he learned over the years to tutor children in our local schools. My work as a Montessori school consultant, and conference speaker, has been enriched by experiencing first-hand how following basic Montessori principles—especially that of protecting deep concentration on activities appropriate for the person's stage of development—and the resulting joy seen in children, is our most important work.

Your Family and Community Today

Many, even those who have never before heard of Montessori education, will recognize themselves with pleasure in this book. There are already families around the world who value spending time with their children above all else, carrying out the daily work together while having conversations and telling stories, and in this way sharing their traditions. They respect their children's choices of what to become interested in, and provide time for concentration and reflection, for making sense of incoming information.

There are teachers who recognize in this book their own intuition to respect choice and concentration, and to give their students opportunities to help with the cleaning and care of the classroom, to solve practical problems, and to have opportunities to help other students with their work.

When we understand human needs and tendencies at different stages of development, prepare an environment that calls forth the best work, and then get out of the way, nature can do the work of creating the complete human being. All the best that the human can be are already within all of us. All of us, and our children, have the potential to be happy, capable, confident, empathetic, hardworking, persistent, and kind human beings with an eye to understanding ourselves, to helping others, and to tackle the problems of the world, which are legion, all of this done in a spirit of joy.

I will end this book with the same quote with which I began it:

> *We shall walk together on this path of life, for all things are a part of the universe, and are connected with each other to form one whole unity. This idea helps the mind of the child to become fixed, to stop wandering in an aimless quest for knowledge.*
>
> *[The child] is satisfied, having found the universal center... with all things.*

OTHER BOOKS IN THIS SERIES

All of these books are interesting and helpful
to parents, teachers, and homeschoolers

The Joyful Child: Montessori,
Global Wisdom for Birth to Three

It is generally agreed by neuroscientists today that 80-85% of
brain growth occurs prenatally and by the end of the third year. This
book supports this growth emotionally, physically, and intellectually
as it is based on the Montessori 0-3, Assistant to Infancy, training. *The
Joyful Child: Montessori, Global Wisdom for Birth to Three* has been
proven to be of value in many ways, including:

(1) Adolescent human development courses

(2) Prenatal classes

(3) University education courses

(4) Montessori 0-3, 3-6, 6-13 teacher training courses

(5) Parent education groups, in person and online

Chapters include:

Part One, The First Year: The Senses; Reaching Out and Grasping;
Sitting up and Working; Crawling, Pulling up, and Standing; Unique
Development and the Child's Self-Respect

Part Two, Age 1-3: Care of Self, Others, and the Environment;
Toys and Puzzles; Music; Language; Art; People; Plants and Animals;
Physical Science and Math

Part Three, The Adult: Preparing the Environment; Parenting and
Teaching

Appendix: How I Weaned Myself (A Child's Perspective);
Comparison of Montessori Assistant to Infancy Practice and Birth-

Three Traditions in Bhutan; Maria Montessori; The Assistant to Infancy Program; About the Author

Birth to Three Resources

Birth to Three development videos often used in presentations based on this book can be found here:
http://www.michaelolaf.net/BirthtoThreeDevelopment.html

Sources of translated versions of this book can be found here:
http://www.michaelolaf.net/JCtranslations.html

Child of the World: Montessori, Global Education for Age 3-12+

This is an overview gained from experience teaching children in Montessori environments at this age, and from our homeschooling experience.

Chapters Include:

Part One, Age 3-6: Caring for Oneself, for Others, and for the Environment; The Preparation and Serving of Food; Toys and Games; The Earth, Physical Sciences; Plants and Animals, Life Sciences; People, Social Sciences; Music and Art; Language; Geometry, Math, and Measurement

Part Two, Age 6-12: Transition to the Elementary Years; The Earth, Physical Sciences; Biology, Life Sciences; The Humanities, Social Sciences; The Arts; Language; Invention, Geometry, and Math

Part Three, Age 0-24: Stages of Development; The Young Adult Age 12-18; The Adult, Age 18-24

Part Four, Parents and Teachers: Preparing a Learning Environment; Parenting and Teaching; Maria Montessori

Homeschooling

The book was written during our homeschooling years as help for parents to understand Montessori practice at this age. Patrick

Farenga, editor of "Growing Without Schooling." Is quoted on the back cover:

> *I have a greater understanding of Montessori education from reading Child of the World than I have gotten from my various other readings about Montessori practice and philosophy. Thank you for centering Montessori principles on the needs of children and families.*

The Red Corolla,
Montessori Cosmic Education
(for age 3-6+)

This book is based on the author's lectures on the 3-6 cultural subjects for an AMI 3-6 course given in Casablanca, Morocco.

Chapters include:

(1) *The Work of the Adult* — creating an album that fills in the gaps in the teacher's general knowledge

(2) *The 3-6 Children's Culture Album* — directions for many practical life, sensorial, and language lessons, in the areas of physics, botany, zoology, history, geography, music, and art

(3) *The leaf collection, and botany classification outline* — including many botanical drawings and explanations on how to begin the work of exploring botany

(4) *Formal Language/Poetry Album* — Directions for creating the beginning of the teacher's language album to be added to year after year

The Red Corolla also contains two articles previously published in Montessori journals:

The Child's Discovery of a Global Vision and a Cosmic Task, from the NAMTA Journal, Vol. 40, No. 2 2015

The Music Environment from the Beginning to the End, from the AMI Journal 2014-2015 Theme Issue "The Montessori Foundations for the Creative Personality"

The Universal Child, Guided by Nature

This is an adaptation of a PowerPoint presentation of the same name given at the 2013 International Montessori Congress in Portland, Oregon. Examples from around the world show that Montessori is based on meeting the human needs for *exploration, movement, work, maximum effort, perfection, concentration*, and *self-control*. Also included is the author's experience in sharing Montessori in new areas of the world and a chapter on how the human needs apply to the adult.

Montessori and Mindfulness

This book is based on a PowerPoint presentation of the same name given at the AMI International Congress in Prague, Czech Republic in 2017. The main point of this book is that, when we put the practice of uninterrupted periods of choice and concentration in the classroom above considerations for covering a specific academic curriculum, that result can be mindfulness, happiness, compassion, love of work, and more.

Chapters include:

Mindfulness; Meditation as a Path to Mindfulness; Montessori and Mindfulness from the Beginning of Life; Mindfulness Support and Impediments (in the Montessori Environment); Flow, the Secret of Happiness; Work as Mindfulness, Mindful Walking; Music as Mindfulness; Mindful Exploration; Born to be Good; Conclusion

Also included is a chapter by Dr. Angeline Lillard, author of Montessori, *The Science Behind the Genius*, entitled "Mindfulness Practiced in Education: Montessori's Approach."

This is the second most translated of my books (after *The Joyful Child*) because it is helpful in improving the lives of not only children, but also parents and teachers.

No Checkmate,
Montessori Chess lessons for Age 3-90+

In this book chess is analyzed in great detail in order to share the steps that can be mastered by children from very young ages, according to their stage of development. This serves as a way to analyze and share other interests and passions of parents with their children.

Chapters include:

How Chess Became a Whole-Family Game; Brief Introduction to Montessori; A Brief Introduction to Chess and How to Use this Book; Chess Grace and Courtesy; Three Levels of Learning Chess; Level I Games; The Amsterdam Chess Museum; Level 2 Games; Level 3 Games; The Question of Competition; The Evolution of Chess, Creativity

Level 1 Games — Preparing the Playing Area; Taking turns; Ending a Game; Moving One Piece

Level 2 Games — Introducing the Concepts of Check and Checkmate; the 3rd Pawn Move; Helping Each Other; Advanced Chess rules; Chess notation, Castling, En passant

Level 3 Games — Trying to Win on One's Own; Cooperative or Non-competitive Board Games; The Benefits of Chess

The Author

Before discovering Montessori Susan first worked as a Latin tutor for high school students, and then as a counselor for girls in a juvenile detention center. She participated in the NAMTA (North American Montessori Teachers Association) research of Montessori environments for adolescents and was the editor of *The Erdkinder Newsletter*. Susan earned Montessori diplomas for 0-3, 2.5-7, and 6-12, worked as a school administrator, and has taught children from age two to thirteen in Montessori environments. She is a school consultant, speaker, and examiner for the Association Montessori Internationale. Susan's children and grandchildren have all attended Montessori schools.

Susan has traveled in more than seventy countries, beginning when she was a sophomore in university. She earned a degree in philosophy at San Francisco State University, a graduate degree in education at Loyola University in Baltimore, and studied *multiple intelligences* under Howard Gardner at Harvard Graduate School of Education. Her website is www.susanart.net

Made in the USA
Columbia, SC
12 February 2022

55352997R00167